From Rock Bottom To Much Success

FROM ROCK BOTTOM TO

MUCH SUCCESS

LARMON CUMMINGS JR

Printed in the United States of America

First Printing, 2020

ISBN: 978-1-7343959-0-7

DEDICATION

I dedicate this book to my wife, Christina, who so faithfully supported me and accepted me with all my faults, even when encouraged to leave by people outside of our relationship who did not understand what it was that we had. You have stayed by my side through so many challenges, and together we made it through. You have been such a great friend, dating all the way back to our high school days working together at Jewel/Osco, and I appreciate having someone like you in my life. Even as we struggled together, juggling school, work, family, through the good times and the bad, you put your faith in me and trusted we would make it through and we did, making us stronger each step of the way. Just know that no matter what happens in the future, I love you, and I will always be here for you for whatever you may need. You are one of the most loyal, and committed persons I have yet to meet in my life, and I thank you from the bottom of my heart for everything you have done for me since we have known one another.

I also dedicate this book to my parents, who have contributed to me growing into the person I am today in a variety of ways. You all have been there when I have been through some of life's most challenging moments, never turning your back on me, even when I thought I knew everything, and being the parents that my peers often wished they had. You created structure in my life, taught me solid morals and values, and though it took me several years to understand what you were teaching me, I can say now that I appreciate you never giving up on me and always forcing me to live up to my potential. I know during my incarceration I really embarrassed you all with the bad decisions I made, and I know you spent numerous challenging nights filled with sadness, hurt, and disappointment, but I vowed to make you proud of me again and be the child you could brag on again, here we are-we did it! I love you all so much, and I am just grateful that the Lord blessed me with parents like you all in my life because I would never have made it to this point I am at right now without your support. Thank you so much.

I want to thank my children, all of my little ladies, for being the motivation I needed to get my act together. Even with you all being so small during so much that took place, I vowed to be a great father to you all, and though I have not perfected fatherhood, just know that I love you all with all my heart, and I have fought so hard just to have you in my life. Being so young you may have not been conscious of what I went through just to be in your lives, but just know it all helped build me into the father you know and love today, and though I may seem over protective at times, maybe reading my story will help you to better understand why. I would never want you all to experience any of the tough times I went through, and I will do my best to protect you all in any way that I am capable of and give you a life filled with love, respect, and commitment to you. Love you all.

To my oldest blood brothers, words can't even express what you all mean to me, and you already know what it is. You all have always had my back, and that still rings true to this very day. Turon, your drive and determination with your business constantly motivates me more than you know, and I am so proud of what you are doing out here. You quit a high paying job to take on your dream of running your own business and you never looked back. You manage your business, your family, and you give back to the community, making it all look so very easy. I've always looked up to you, especially with us being so close in age, and I just look forward to witnessing the legacy that you continue to build each and every day. Love you bro. Cory, man big bro, I've always looked up to you and it was like as much trouble you caused growing up, you couldn't do any wrong in my eyes. Watching you go from that wild kid growing up and transitioning into the legit life, getting married, taking care of your family, it really motivated me that it was all possible. We both beat the odds and did not return to the prison system, even when so many people doubted us both, and I just look forward to what successes and opportunities life has in store for you. To my oldest sister Toya, whether you knew this or not, but growing up you were one of the smartest people I knew. Seeing you grow up, go to college, get those great jobs, live in those big houses, and lead a lifestyle that so many people could only dream of, that motivated me so much and I thank you for showing me what was possible when you put your mind to it and never let the obstacles prevent you from accomplishing your goals. You helped me realize that I did not have to take such severe risks with my life in order to have success, and you showed me that all I had to do was educate myself, and with knowledge, anything was possible.

To my other family and friends, who have always had my back- Nate, Terrence, Don, just to name a close few, just want to take the time to say thank you brothers, and I appreciate everything you've done for me. We have been through some rough times, had a lot of fun, and it has all built us into some very strong men and I just love seeing you all successful in your various paths that you have chosen to walk in life. From helping support my kids while I was away, to the visits, money you sent, being there when I came home and helping me through the tough times, just know that I appreciate it all and that is why we are brothers for life and I love you all. I've watched us all grow up from immature kids getting into all sorts of trouble, to positive, mature, strong black men taking care of our families and being positive role models in our community. To my other friend Stephanie, we came all the way from studying late for those SXU projects, making it happen in the midst of all the challenges we faced trying to balance work and school, we did it! Meeting you in those classes introduced me unknowingly to one of my best friends, and since then you have helped me through some of the very challenging times I faced in my life, encouraging me to keep going even when the thoughts of quitting crossed my mind. You have been the true definition of what a friend is supposed to be, and I just thank you for everything. So much love to you.

To all of my professors I have met along the way, mentors in life and business, classmates, and others I've crossed paths with over the years, I want to thank you for giving me knowledge, giving me strength, and motivating me to keep going in the midst of the barriers that I faced. Some of you even knew my testimony, but that was good because you never treated me any differently. You respected me for who I was, never having any biases on where I came from, what I had been through, and I really do thank you for that. I also want to thank all of those who did NOT think I would make it. I want to thank all of those companies that did not want to give me a chance to show what I was capable of accomplishing, because had you done that I may be stuck in a job right now and never taken a chance on myself and pursued my dreams. There were so many people who painted me as another statistic, saying my life was pretty much so over, and there would be no opportunity for an ex con like myself. Hearing those biases and negative statements come from family, some who I once considered friends, professors, classmates, etc., I can honestly say it motivated me so much to prove you wrong. I used that negativity to keep pushing me each day, even more so when things got difficult, so I thank you all as well for your contribution to my success.

Last, but certainly not least, I want to thank another one of my very good friends Jasma. You challenged me to stop prolonging writing this book, and you worked with me each step of the way to not only get started, but to see it all the way through to the finish line. We go all the way back to high school, and even then you had my back, always being a true friend. I want to thank you so much for working with me on this project, keeping me encouraged, and also being rough on me when I strayed off into the realm of procrastination. You are a great coach, and

I know your business will continuously be blessed because you have a very pure heart, always doing for others without expecting anything in return oftentimes, and that is exactly why God continues to bless you and your family. Just know I appreciate all of the time you have put into this project with me, giving me your honest feedback, letting me be creative and just write what was on my mind, and guiding me so that I could get to this point of completion. We did it! So much love for you Jazzy.

FOREWORD

LARMON CUMMINGS

Encountering many young African American males as a function of my chosen profession, I've become accustomed to listening to a variety of life stories from my young brothers depending on the circumstances under which we've met.

Discounting for the moment that as a corporate small business liaison officer, I mostly see entrepreneurial types, many with the passion it takes to succeed in running their own businesses. These men approach me to discuss specific opportunities with the Fortune 100 Company that I work for. Their guile and nimble approaches are always impressive but rarely unique. This book outlines a story that is both impressive and unique.

Actualizing my passion for volunteering in situations, with the idea of influencing young African American males to be positive impactors of their own lives is a central theme of this foreword. The aforementioned path defines my very intentional and yet happenstance meeting of Larmon Cummings.

To wit; I have always served in several volunteer ministries of my Church, The Salem Baptist Church of Chicago. Additionally I actively seek speaking opportunities to share my personal insights on life and success formulas for the urban focused. In other words, I want to engage in straight talk with folks that grew up like I did and make plain that there are no mysteries in finding a good life. When presented an opportunity to serve as an adjunct professor of Business at Chicago State University (CSU), by a former Northwestern Professor of mine who was the Dean of the CSU School of Business, the decision was a no brainer. It fit my professional profile as well as my personal altruistic agenda of helping urban students that were in many cases under resourced.

Larmon was enrolled in one of my first advanced management classes. Noteworthy of those 24 students in this class of juniors and seniors, 11 were males. It was encouraging to see that many young black males in an advanced business class. Larmon was an engaged and highly energized student from the very beginning, requiring no warm up to establishing himself as a superior communicator among his peers. I only mention this because I believe it was significant relative to what was to unfold. We forged a relationship that was uniquely ours, professor to student, man to man, elder Christian to evolving Christian.

He will tell his story far better and so much more compelling in the chapters to come, but in penning this foreword, an honor for which I was beyond touched, observing the journey of this young brother, barely into his 20's put me on notice and recalibrated what I thought I knew about young black men.

The transparent teaching style of sharing my own experiences and values in order to relate to my students was causal to Larmon pulling me aside early in the semester with the simple asking of "Can we just talk one day about life?" There was much on his mind that it became clear he had not had the chance to share with any older black male, or at least not one with the stark contrast of my personal history or current stature as an accomplished professional. Our encounter was about his vision of self; his burning intent to overcome an adult life kick off that like too many young men included incarceration, teen fatherhood, and various other social missteps.

The joy, if not amazement of writing the preview of this story embodies a restraint of emotions, witnessing the fullness in short context in which Larmon Cummings, simply willed his life into betterment. Incarceration, teen fatherhood, in many cases defines the path for black men. In this case, the book outlines a triumphant cadence of reclaiming life, involving marrying the mother of his children, earning a degree, post incarceration, and launching not one but two successful entrepreneurial endeavors that completely support his family. More importantly he continually claims a fierce commitment to his Christian values, openly and often declaring his belief in the heavenly father.

This story is simple, and in its simplicity outlines a "can do" message that young men fighting back the condescending messages and images that all too often have been thrust into their faces as prophecy, a story of truth and connectivity to an achievable if not desirable reality.

Emmett T. Vaughn

TABLE OF CONTENTS

INTRODUCTION

This book was inspired by God to bring encouragement to individuals who may have been directly or indirectly affected by the consequences that come along with living life in the streets. This book speaks not only to the people who have made bad decisions at some point in their life by being involved in the street life, and it also speaks to the family, friends, and associates of those individuals as well because they are also affected by the consequences. Those bad decisions often times result in being introduced to the prison system, and this can be a very challenging experience for all parties involved. I will use my story to illustrate that the individual being incarcerated is not the only one who has to endure this challenging time, but it also strongly affects the family just as much.

As I looked back on my earlier years in my life, I wanted to use my personal experiences to show that no matter what social class you come from, neighborhood, or what trials and tribulations that you face growing up; you can use that as your motivation to push you towards having success in your life. Instead of using the barriers as excuse to explain failure, you can use those same barriers to create strength and motivation within you to continue pressing forward not matter how difficult things may seem. A lot of times the area a person grows up in can put them in a position in life without the hope of being able to have a vision of anything different. I want to eliminate that train of thought.

In writing this book, I especially want to speak to the young men of color who look up to the street life and see it as some glamorous way of living. I want to show them through my own personal experiences that the life is not as glamorous as it may appear to them, and I want to show some of the consequences that come along with it. Often times young men, as I once was, are greatly influenced by the older men in our neighborhoods, the music we listen to, movies and TV shows we watch, and I just want to express how important it is to be conscious of this because it will really have a strong influence on them growing up.

I want this book to show how the justice system often times does not provide much justice at all, but largely has a very biased position towards specific races and cultural backgrounds in this country, that especially being minorities. Often times race forces you to face much harsher penalties than other races that commit the same crimes. This also creates a cycle that is intended to keep an individual repeating a lot of the same mistakes due to a lack of opportunity caused from the biased treatment in the American justice system. A lack of job opportunities, denial of housing, and a limited number of programs to assistant with a reintroduction to society upon being released from prison are sure to create barriers to an individual on a path to redemption.

As I go through how my upbringing led me to make a lot of the decisions in my life, I want to illustrate how important it is to have a strong support system. Sometimes people may not have the positive family members, friends, or people in their lives, so in this book I give suggestions on some ways you can build this support system by going outside of your comfort zone and finding comfort in entering new societies that have more positive figures in it. I show how important this can be in helping to keep a person motivated to learn new concepts about life, and having people around that can help assist in incorporating these new concepts into your own lives. I also explain some important parts of adulthood that people should always be conscious of such as building their credit, saving, among other important principles. After reading this book, I want people to be motivated to go after their goals, never letting anyone deter them, no matter what they have been through in life.

CHAPTER 1: THE LAST DROP

As I'm driving on the expressway my heart is beating fast. You would think after all of my times on the road, running drugs out of town, I would be more relaxed than I was. I am doing my best to seem as inconspicuous as possible. I have my hands 10 and 2 on the steering wheel, seat belt on tight, driving sitting up straight with my eyes on the road and in my side mirrors. Seems like every other mile I drive I see a state trooper sitting off to the side of the road or driving slowly behind me, only to speed right past me. My nerves are shot to say the least. While I was at work earlier, doing yet another tire rotation and oil change, I told myself this would be the "last" drop I make to this dude. This "last" drop was going to set me straight for a while. Yeah, the money working this apprenticeship is slow, but once I finish my degree things will be better. This "last" drop would give me a cushion financially so I wouldn't have to stress over this minimum wage paycheck that I seem to work for so hard every week. "Have patience, slow down son-you're trying to get to where your dad and I am at in life overnight and it took us several years to get here," my mom always used to tell me. I am just thinking of this precious baby girl I just had, and just thinking of all the stuff she needed in life. On top of that, I had my second daughter 6 months following her birth, so things had really gotten serious in my life. The cost of milk, diapers, and clothes, none of it was getting any cheaper. I know I told my boys I was done selling drugs and out the game. I was done playing in these streets. I got accepted into this automotive apprenticeship and I was going to do things the right way now.

Earlier that summer, the police had busted one of the guys working for me running drugs. After he made a pickup from me heading out of town, one of his friends threw a Burger King bag out of the window and they were pulled over. The police searched their car, found the drugs I had given him, and they all were arrested. That was the last run he made for me, and after I gave him the drugs I didn't hear from him for a while. Now he owed me a decent amount of money for that shipment, so I was very pissed to say the least. The fact that I was calling him repeatedly and he never responded back, that was very unusual of him. After so long of trying to catch up with him and not being able to locate him, I took it not only as a loss, but as a sign that it was time for me to quit playing in this dirty game, and get focused on doing the right thing for my baby girl. This is when I made the decision to stop selling drugs for good and just focus on school, working in the apprenticeship, and taking care of my family. Little did I know that this same guy would be the one to set me up, and change my life forever. Several months had passed since I heard from him, and one day he had called me up. He explained the situation with him getting arrested and how it all went down, told me that he would never run off like that owing me money after all I had done for him, and he was now back on his feet making moves, had the money he owed me, and was ready to get back to work. He had met a new contact out of town in WI looking for a cocaine connect, and he told him about me and how I always had some weight. I met up with my guy because I definitely wanted to get the money he owed me, and I had no intentions of doing any more business with him, I mean, I was out of the game trying to focus on doing positive stuff at this point.

When I met up with the guy to pick up my money he owed me, we started discussing this new contact he had met. I explained to him that I was out of the game and focusing on my family and my future right now, I was not interested in going back down that path. He explained to me that the cocaine prices in the Wisconsin area his contact told him about were much higher than what we were getting here, and it would be a great opportunity. "Just meet with him once to hear him out, if you didn't like it then just leave", he said. He really expressed that it was worth at least hearing him out. As I continued listening to him, it was a mental battle going on in my head. Do I stick it out with the job and school, and keep my word in saying that I was done, or do I give this some more thought and hear him out? This could be my "last" run I thought, put a few months in, get paid, and really get out of the life for good. I mean, that minimum wage I was making in the dealership definitely was not helping guide my decision in doing the right thing. I was used to making money and not struggling financially, I mean good money, so I made the decision to hear him out. My mind was pretty much so made up, why I was even fooling myself; back to the game I went.

As I got closer to the meet up spot, my phone started ringing. My mom is calling me saying that for some reason she was thinking about me earlier that day, and she just had a bad feeling and needed me to come to the house right away to talk with her. I tell her ok, I was on my way to take care of some "business" right quick and would come that way when I finished up. She was not going for it that easy, she kept emphasizing that she needed me to come right away, she really needed to see me. I told her that I was driving and needed to get off my phone so I didn't get a ticket, I would call her once I finished up. I hung up the phone feeling even more nervous, like damn, what was all of that about. I was already feeling sort of thrown off because my girlfriend Shelly kept telling me to come get her so she could ride with me. She had a bad feeling about this particular run, and she would feel better if she were with me. I kept telling her that I didn't have time to wait for her. I had everything already set up and it wouldn't take me long. I mean, I had been making this run for almost 2 months now to this guy; it was in and out-easy money. Only difference this time was that I was bringing way more drugs then I did on any of the other runs.

I finally get to my exit and head to the meeting spot. I call the guy and let him know that I am close. He explains that things didn't seem right at the usual spot, so he went across the street to this parking lot in front of a large strip mall. I was already feeling so nervous about this whole trip, so this didn't make me feel any better. To make things worse, I had just purchased the new Beanie Sigel album out at the time and the track "Feel It in the Air" was playing on my cd player. Now, the song is about a guy selling drugs and being setup by someone he trusted-he could "feel it in the air." That definitely just made me start thinking about turning around and getting right back on the expressway and going home. My gut was screaming something didn't feel right, and to just go back home. It was like when you see people on TV with the angel on one shoulder and the devil on the other. The angel was telling me to get out of there, and the devil kept reminding me about the payday right in front of me. The drop off was simple, it always went smooth, so go get the money and make it happen. Thinking back now, I really do hate that little devil.

As I am sitting in my car off to the side of the road thinking about what I should do next, my contact I was meeting kept calling my phone. The first two times he called me I ignored the call, I was still in deep thought. This was my last chance to make the decision to leave if that was what I was going to do, but in the back of my mind the money kept reminding me of why I was even here in the first place. Mentally, I tell the angel on my left shoulder to shut up, and I drive across the street to make it happen. As I drive into the parking lot, things just seemed to really slow down and it was as if time started to barely go by. It was as if people were walking in slow motion, and I was not able to shake this knot in the pit of my stomach. The guy calls me again and I answer, "where you at?" he says. As I am talking to him on the phone, I am suspiciously watching everyone moving around me, really trying to get a feel for the situation. I am doing my best to locate his car, trying to see if I see anything out of place. After circling around the parking lot a couple of times I pull into the parking spot next to where he is parked. I reach around to the back seat to grab the baby bag I was carrying the drugs in. I grab the bag and I tell him to come jump in my car. He was on the phone talking with someone, so for the sake of time I just got out and headed towards his car. Now I would usually carry my gun on these runs to protect myself, but dealing with him over the last couple of months had me get too comfortable, and I figured didn't need it anymore after our first few meetups.

I opened up the passenger door to his car and get into the front passenger seat. I put the bag on the floor in between my legs. He was still on the phone talking with someone, and at that point I signaled for him to hang up. I mean, it's not like we have all the time in the world- let's make it happen and get out of here! The guy gets off the phone and he asks me if I brought everything. I tell him yeah, and I ask him if he had the money. He said he did, so I told him let's do this so we could get out of there. Now, from our last few times meeting we had gained somewhat of a rapport/trust for one another, so the drops were fast and simple. I brought the order he put in, he brought the cash, the exchange was made and we both went our separate ways. We stopped taking the time to weigh up the drugs I brought, count the money, I mean, we started doing constant business with each other so there had to be some level of trust established if this was going to work. Over all the time we dealt with each other there was never a short on money, nor was there a short on the drugs I delivered-it was always all there on both sides. With that being said, it threw me off when he requested that he wanted to weigh everything up this time. I now turned my body and faced him, my back turned halfway towards the passenger side window, and I asked why did he need to weigh it up all of a sudden? What, he didn't trust me after all of the business we had done up to this point? I was insulted to say the least, and I made sure he knew this. He explained that since this was the biggest order up to this point, he just wanted to ensure that everything was everything since there was so much money at stake this time. Furious, but understanding his position, I said ok. I mean, if I were in his shoes I would do the same thing; you definitely cannot trust people in this particular line of work to say the least. I told him that before we started weighing up anything, he needed to show me the money. He said ok, and he started to reach around to the back seat to get the bag.

Now, at this point there were a variety of different emotions that I was feeling. There were so many thoughts going through my mind. Did he really have the money? Then came excitement, was this really happening? Damn I was about to be paid. Was this a stickup? Damn, why didn't I bring my gun, what was I thinking. I was definitely nervous, seemed like that knot in my stomach turned into a truckload of bricks at this point. I was kind of pissed because we were even going through all of this nonsense, in a car parked in the damn parking of this strip mall with all of these people moving around. Why didn't I just leave and go back home? I felt so stupid for even being here. As he was reaching around to grab the money, my eyes were completely focused on him and all of his movements. I mean, if he was trying to pull something I was definitely going to be ready. Then my mind started thinking in another direction, why would he try to pull something like that in such a busy area like this? After these types of thoughts racing through my mind I started to dismiss the idea of a robbery. Who would be so dumb as to pull something like that in such a busy area like this? We were in Hinsdale, IL at the end of the day, one of the richest suburbs in the state, so causing all of that attention wouldn't even make sense. As I am thinking all of these thoughts I never take my eyes off of him, and I actually start reaching for the bag with one hand and the door handle with the other without even thinking. I had been playing in the game long enough where I think my instincts just took over and were preparing me an escape route just in case. As I am watching him reaching for this bag, I hear a loud BANG on the window! Damn I thought, this is how my life ends. Where did I go wrong? Well, let me tell you about my life, about how it all started, how I arrived at this exact location I was at right then and there. This is where I came from.

CHAPTER 2: THIS IS WHERE

I CAME FROM

I am the youngest of 4 children. I have a sister who is the oldest, and two older brothers. My oldest brother and sister are about a year and some months apart, then my parents waited about 4 years until they had my brother and I. My parents worked a lot, both usually keeping about 2 jobs each to support us, so my older sister was usually the one left in charge to watch over us. This would present a challenge for her because she was still young herself, but it was also a bit of a challenge trying to watch after 3 boys, all of whom were always full of energy. My parents would leave early in the morning to head to work, then would not return until later in the evening, so during the day when we were not in school we would be with her the majority of the day. With my older brother and sister being so close in age, they frequently would get into fights with each other. My older brother felt he was old enough and didn't have to take orders from her, so they would argue and he would end up leaving. This was how things usually went between the two of them.

My older brother was usually in trouble, whether it was in school, in the house, or just out in the neighborhood with the police. He was just that type of kid. He was the type of kid that didn't like taking orders, and he pretty much so liked to do his own thing. There were always court dates that my parents had to go to. The school was always calling my parents because he was acting up in school, so that led to more detentions, suspensions, and eventually led to him getting kicked out of school. With my other brother and I being so much younger than he was, we always looked up to him. We thought he was so cool for being such a rebel, and though we were scared at the time to misbehave like he did, we definitely started acting out more and more. With my parents not being around during the day much because of work, we slowly started to venture out and explore what the streets had to offer.

My parents at some point during their marriage had discovered the religion of Jehovah's Witnesses, and they believed very strongly in their viewpoints and religious beliefs, so they felt raising their family this way was what would be best for us. They had discovered this before their two youngest kids were born, so I was raised in this religion from birth and it was all I knew. This particular religion was very strict on how they wanted their members to conduct themselves, and this definitely had an impact on how I would later view the idea of "religion" and also God. There were no birthdays, or any other holidays for that matter, to be celebrated. There was bible study on Wednesday every week, and every Sunday we went to the Kingdom Hall for what seemed like several hours. This was the equivalent of other religions going to a church. I was never around any profanity, or any other behavior that would be deemed unsatisfactory, and my siblings and I were very rarely allowed to associate with people outside of our religion. They felt that if you prevented your family from associating with individuals outside of the belief, then that would help you maintain order in your household, and this was the best route to raising your children. Being older and more knowledgeable now, I can see why they felt this way. It was more to protect your children from being distracted by other worldly desires, but I just felt like they restricted too much, so a lot of kids in the religion naturally rebelled.

With my parents working so many hours everyday, and my sister being the only real adult supervision at the house, my older brother's influence started to affect my other brother and I much more. We started hanging out on our block with him and the other older guys much more, and now the gangs started to be more appealing. I mean, the gangs really just consisted of the guys who stayed on your block, so in our minds we weren't really doing anything that bad. The block we stayed on there just happen to be a lot of kids around the same age range. We had the older kids who were pretty much so most of the smaller kids' older siblings on the block. We then had the kids that were sort of in the middle, like my brother and I, and lastly, we had the younger kids. We would always get into fights with the other guys from other "sets", which at the time was pretty much so guys who just lived on different blocks in the area. With our older brothers though, since they were driving and riding the bus to different places all around the city, they would get into fights in many different areas, so things were way more serious for them. At the time I was still one of the smaller kids, so it was just fun hanging out, fighting the other kids from different blocks, then we all pretty much so still hung out playing basketball, football, and baseball with each other. To us that was fun. The thing a lot of us had in common was that most of our parents worked a lot to support us, so there wasn't always a lot of adult supervision; the older kids pretty much so raised us. With most of the families consisting of 4-5 kids, those were a lot of kids to feed, so our parents working blue collar jobs had to put in a lot of time to make it work. Some of my friends only lived with their mom, or even grandparents, so things were harder on some. We always looked out for each other though, our block was our family. The older kids walked the younger kids to school every day, and when they got into fights, we fought right alongside them. During the mid 1990's things started getting much worse though in the city of Chicago. There started to be more violence, more shootings, more drugs being sold, and it became even more important for us to stick together.

The more my older brother got into trouble, the more stress I would see my parents endure. They would constantly go back and forth to court with him, and it got so bad that he was sent to the juvenile detention center. I could see how much it affected my parents, and even more so my dad because he was working so much, I think he believed it was his fault because he was not able to spend very much time with us. My mother had decided to leave her job and took a job as a crossing guard at our school. I guess they felt this way there would be someone home with us more to monitor what we were doing, and try to prevent my other brother and I from going in the wrong direction. With my mother taking a major income reduction, this only made my dad work harder. Aside from working 12-14 hour days at the steel mill he worked at, he would also do plumbing jobs on the side as well. To spend more time with us, my dad started taking my brother and I on jobs with him. We were still pretty young, so we really didn't do much while we were there. We would hand him tools, get stuff from the work truck, and at the end of every job he would give us some money. It was not a lot of money, but to us it was like we were rich! This really started to open my eyes up for the first time to working and making money for myself, and also opened my eyes up to the benefits of owning your own business.

As my dad worked at the steel mill, he realized the need to spend more time with my brother and I, so he started cutting back some on the hours at the mill, and he made up for it by doing more plumbing work since he had been getting more referrals and the business was growing very rapidly. With the Jehovah Witness community being so tight and only really associating with other members in the faith, they used a lot of the same contractors when they needed work done and really did not venture outside of their own people much. This allowed my dad to get referred for a lot of business, and this meant my brother and I going on more jobs with my dad and spending more time with him, which in turn meant us making more money. With us having a large family, my dad did his best to expose us to things some of my friends on our block didn't get to experience with their family. We always went on some sort of trip out of town every year, mainly roads trips since he had bought a brand new conversion van. He really used his resources to try and spend as much time with my brother and I as possible. My sister at this point had already graduated high school and went off to college. My older brother was locked up, so with his last two sons he really tried to do things differently.

The majority of my dad's side of the family is spread across the state of Michigan, so we would take several road trips back and forth there throughout the year visiting his side of the family. During the summer to get us out of the city and give us a change of pace, my dad would send my brother and I up there to stay with our family for several weeks. This is when I was first exposed to my uncle who also had his own business. He would build houses from the ground up, live in them for like 2 years, sell them, and then build another house, usually larger than the one before it. We would help him build the houses when we came to visit. Since we were still fairly young, it consisted more of us just helping him, similar to what we did with our dad. He would also pay us money and we would be so excited. This showed us another male figure in our family, running his own business, and making some good money doing it. My uncle had a brand new corvette, big house, and a beautiful family. Aside from the construction company, he also owned a successful landscaping business that he ran with one of my other uncles. With this particular uncle we would also tag along and help out. It was so much fun to us riding the lawn mowers, out in the country cutting the yards of these huge homes, and just the idea of being on our own time without anyone to answer to really intrigued me. I also noticed that this uncle seemed to have it all as well. He had a nice home, brand new Ford Mustang, motorcycles, snowmobiles, you name it. I watched and admired my uncle's more than they probably ever realized, and this really started to teach me a strong work ethic and made me realize how hard work would pay off if I put my energy and efforts into my own business. My brother and I would have so much fun visiting my family in Michigan, and it was always so hard to leave. It was like my cousins there had it made in our mind, really living the good life, but to them they looked up to us just as much. We were more like the cool kids from the big city of Chicago, and it didn't help much that we had that same rebellious attitude when we came there, so they thought we were such tough guys. We would bully some of the country kids that lived out by them, especially if any of our cousins said they had a problem with them. Anytime they had issues with the local kids, they would always threaten them, "I'm going to get my cousins from Chicago", and then people would leave them alone. They would always talk about how the family said we got into so much trouble back in Chicago, and that's why they sent us there to Michigan. We had so much fun together and when the summer was over and it was time to go home, I always came home with a pocket full of money that I saved from working with my uncles. This was my second exposure to small business.

Life in the city was different than being in the country back in Michigan, life in the city moved at a much faster pace. The desire to have all of the latest fashion was very popular in our community. As I was getting older, when I would start back to school, the desire to fit in, as a young man grew increasingly strong. I wanted the nice clothes and shoes my friends were wearing, and my eyes started to desire more "things" that cost a lot of money at the time. With my dad working hard to support his family, he did his best to get us a lot of stuff, but there came a point where we started wanting more than he was willing to give. He told us he was not buying us a pair of gym shoes that cost $150; he worked too hard for his money. He would buy us a good pair of shoes, a good set of clothes to wear, and if what he could afford wasn't good enough for us, then we would have to work and earn our own money to buy what we wanted since our tastes were so expensive. That conversation my dad and I had that day changed the way I viewed things going forward. From that day forward I vowed that I would buy my own shoes, my own clothes, and I knew what I had to do to get them. I was too young at the time to get a job, so I knew I would have to work hard for my money, just like I seen my dad and my uncles do. I would ask my dad to go on more plumbing jobs with him to earn more money. In the summer I would cut the neighbors grass, the fall I would rake leaves, and in the winter I would shovel snow with my brother. We would make so much money walking through the neighborhood shoveling snow, and would be so excited as we laid our earnings across the bed and counted to see who made the most. My brother would spend his money just as quickly as he made it, but not me. I would always save my money and hide it somewhere in the house where no one could ever find it. The thrill I got from seeing the money add up was so exciting. My brother would always call me cheap because I would never want to spend my money on the stuff like he did, but he always knew I kept some money somewhere hidden. This allowed me the opportunity to start buying the more expensive clothes and shoes I wanted, and this made me want to get more money because now I wanted more "stuff".

On my mother's side of the family, I had some family members that also had their own businesses, but these businesses were not like my family in Michigan, no, these made way more money, and at the age I was at during that point in my life when I started to become aware of their businesses, these business ventures started to really get my full undivided attention. These particular family members would always have the latest fashions, nice jewelry, and they always kept beautiful women around them. They drove really nice cars, and they always had a pocket full of money. As a young man who was already starting to get an appetite for nice things, and my hormones making me constantly thinking about pretty women, I started to become intrigued about how their particular businesses worked. What did they really do every day to live like they did? Every time we had family functions it was like they always were just living so good, like they didn't have a care in the world. I really admired them and looked up to them; this is how I wanted to live.

The more I started to watch my other family members and how they lived, I started to compare their lifestyles to my family on my dad's side. Yeah, they made good money, but it seemed like they worked so hard for it, and it seemed like they really didn't have the time to enjoy it. When I looked on the other side, they always seemed to have all the time in the world, they traveled a lot, and they just seemed to always have a lot of fun. They were young, and to me, from what I could see from the outside looking it, they didn't have a care in the world. That was how I wanted to live in my mind. It seemed like working hard was "alright", but I wanted to find out what this side of the family did because life seemed to definitely be more exciting for them. From being on my block, hanging with some of the older guys, I was already familiar with the lifestyle of selling drugs. I used to watch my brother bag up drugs in the house when my parents were gone, but at that time

I really was not interested. It just seemed like a waste of time to me. Watching my older brother and other family on the block sell drugs, at that point I think I was more interested in working hard for my money like my dad and uncles, selling drugs did not really seem like the way I wanted to go. At this point though in my life, seeing the rewards of selling drugs on this level, well, now that lifestyle had my attention. I thought they were some of the coolest guys on the planet and I wanted to be like them so bad.

CHAPTER 3: TIME TO HUSTLE

I got my first official job at the age of 15 years old at Popeye's Chicken. I was in my second year of high school and I figured it was time for me to start earning some extra money to add to what I was already making doing the plumbing with my dad, cutting grass, raking leaves, and whatever else I was doing to make money. When I started high school I started playing football, so that started to take away some of the free time that I had to earn some extra money doing some of the other jobs. The way I seen it, I could play football, work the job, then go on the plumbing jobs with my dad when I had some free time to do so. When I first got hired I was so excited, I felt it was finally time for me to really start making some big money, or at least that's what I thought at the time. At that particular time, the minimum wage in IL was $5.15/hr, so the reality of the job was that it definitely was not going to bring in as much money as I imagined it would, but with it being my first job I was still excited. This would be my first job that I not only got on my own, but as a teenage boy, it came with a sense of pride for me. The old feelings of watching my dad and my uncles work hard and earn a good living really impressed upon me at that time. I felt like I was a man, and I could really support myself if I wanted to. At that point in my life I had already been buying the majority of my clothes and shoes. My parents still would purchase those items, but at the time they weren't what I wanted, so I really did not even wear them. I wanted to be fly, and the items that I wanted were expensive. As I mentioned before, I was a dedicated saver, so I always kept a stash of cash hidden around the house from doing my odd end jobs. I was like my mother; she always emphasized the importance of saving my money, and not spending everything that came in. I can honestly say that still lives with me today.

When I started this job, I already spoke with my manager and let him know that I was playing football, so I was only able to work a certain number of hours each week. I would work 2-3 days for about 4-6 hours each day. I would take the bus from school, get dropped off close by my job, then walk the rest of the way. I would go to work right after football practice, so I was usually very tired after going to school all day, then practice for 2-3 hours, then go to work. The thing that shocked me the most was that the first day I started that job I realized I hated it. They would have me frying chicken, and in the process the grease would always splash onto my skin burning me and leaving red burns all over my arms. It also gave me very bad acne due to me being around all of the grease. I did like the fact that I could eat all of the food I wanted, and being a growing young man playing sports, I definitely had an endless appetite. The first paycheck I received came the second week from me working there. I was so excited that whole week just anticipating getting my first check, I was going to deposit this fat check into the bank and I was going to be paid is what I thought. The day I my first check was cut I did not have to work that day, so I came up to the place after school. I could not wait to get out of school that day, it was payday and it was Friday. My weekend was about to be awesome I thought. When I came to pick up that first check, the manager had all of the payroll checks in a box lined up nice and neat. Everyone was getting paid today, I just knew everyone was just as excited as I was, and if they weren't who cared, I was living the dream I thought. I worked what seemed to be forever and now it was time to reap the fruits of my labor. When I got outside I quickly opened the envelope and when I seen the check amount my whole demeanor changed. This couldn't be right I thought, so I went back into the place to talk to the manager. I explained that not only was my check about $64, but they took money out for some stuff that I didn't even authorize them to take out. She explained that these items were things such as taxes, medical, etc., and the state was required to take them out from everyone, also the cost of my uniform. This couldn't be right I thought. I worked so hard those last two weeks, and all I was going to take home was around $50! This sucked! How did these people here survive I thought? Some of the people working there were twice my age, a couple of people even older than that. This definitely was not going to work I thought. At that moment I knew I had to do something else to make some real money.

Watching my dad and uncles run their own small businesses and work hard to support each of their families, it really instilled a great work ethic in me and I did not mind keeping a job to bring in extra money. The challenge I faced at this point in my life was finding a job that brought in what I deemed to be a respectable income. At that time in my life I knew that the jobs available to me would never bring in the income I was looking for, so I knew I had to do something extra on the side to generate some money in addition to working a job. Watching some of the older guys in my life as I was growing up, I noticed they were very flashy, and they really made it be known that they were selling drugs. The cops knew it, the neighbors knew it, and the streets knew it. As I was contemplating getting involved with this lifestyle, I made the decision that I would not take that route. These particular guys were always being harassed by the police, and they always were in and out of jail. There was the other guys I watched though, whom I knew had money, but they moved much differently than the other guys. These guys had car washes, laundromats, car lots, owned real estate, etc., so to people on the outside looking in they could never really tell they sold drugs. I would later learn that owning these types of businesses were important because that's how they "washed" their money, which basically meant taking the illegal drug money and cycling it through various legal businesses to make the money legit. These were the guys I started paying closer attention to. They reminded me of the rapper Jay-Z, who was another very influential person in my life growing up. He had the rare story of growing up in the projects selling drugs, and making it in the rap industry to become very successful, and most importantly, he became very rich and he was now legit. I listened to his music very closely and the more I listened, the more I wanted that story for my life. I wanted to be the dope boy that made his own way, and in the future be able to not only make it and be successful, but I wanted to bring on my close friends and family so they could share in the same success. I made the decision that I was going to start off slow; I was not going to get ahead of myself. Since my oldest brother was serving an 8yr sentence in the Federal Correctional Facility at the time, I could not use his help to get started. What I did have was relationships with a lot of his friends that looked after me while he was away, and they were like big brothers to me as well. There were a few that I had a pretty close relationship with and I knew they sold weed, so I made the decision to reach out to them, I was going to be the new weed man in town.

When I first approached one of my brother's friends about supplying me the weed I was going to sell, he refused. He explained to me what came along with hustling, and he knew I was very smart not only inside school but also outside, so he didn't want to be the cause of me getting caught up in some trouble. I explained to him that I would be ok and I was grown enough to make my own decisions, so spare me the lecture. I mean, at this point in my life I was a 16 year old with all of the answers. I pretty much so knew everything there was to know, and I definitely was not trying to hear a speech from someone who actually started selling drugs earlier than me. After us going back and forth discussing this, he told me that he would try me out. He was under the impression that I wanted him to front me the drugs, but I told him no, I had my own money that I had been saving and I didn't want to owe him anything. I started off small and made my first purchase, I was now a drug dealer. I was so excited, but I was also nervous at the same time. I told myself that I had to be smart if I was going to avoid getting caught up by the police, or even risk having one of the stick up guys rob me. I called up my best friends and they met up with me to come see what I had. By the time they met up with me I had already went to the store and purchased a scale and some baggies, I was serious about making that money and I was not about to wait around to get started. When my guys came by I had already started breaking down the couple of ounces that I bought into smaller nickel and dime bags. As I think back now, I feel so ashamed of how disrespectful I was setting up in my parent's house like I did. I showed no shame in using their house as a drug spot, and later on it would come back to haunt me. When my guys walked into the basement and seen my setup I could tell by the look on their faces that they were impressed. We had all talked about it so many times, but I was the first one to actually follow through on it. I could tell they had a new level of respect for me, and they even jumped in and started helping me bag up the rest of my package. I felt like I was the man.

I had quit my first job at Popeye's Chicken after a little over a month. It seemed like I was working so many hours and the paycheck just never added up at the end of the week. Between me playing football and going to school, it seemed like I never had much time for myself, and I figured if I was going to give up that much of my free time, it had definitely better pay off more than this was. The age I was at I really did not care much to give any 2-week notice to my manager. I picked up my last check and told him that I was not going to be able to work there any longer because it was affecting my school and me playing football. He did not mind much, I mean, it was like a revolving door in that place with so many people coming in and out. I did like hanging out with this one Mexican guy who worked there though, we used to sneak out back and smoke weed when the manager would go home for the night. We both had been talking about quitting, so it was no surprise when I told him I was leaving. He sold weed at the time, so we used to talk about that as well when we worked together. He said he was probably going to leave as well, but I came to find out that he had been saying that for the last 2 years he worked there, so I just figured he liked the place. I knew I had to find another job soon, especially if I was going to start selling weed. I had to have some type of legit job so people did not question where I was getting my money. I started filling out a lot of applications to different places, but I made the decision that I would never work in fast food again-I hated it! I ended up getting a call from Jewel/Osco and they wanted me to come in for an interview. I was pretty excited about this job because they started your pay off at close to $8.50/hr. and it was also along the bus route home from my school, so I could get dropped off after football practice during the season. It was as if things were all just falling perfectly in place for me.

I ended up doing very well on my interview with Jewel and got hired on the spot, so that was great news for me. My parents were so excited for me as well, they thought I was really doing great. I was doing great playing football, I hardly ever asked them for much because I usually had my own money, I was going to school, and they were proud of me. I would get in my occasional trouble here and there in school and in the neighborhood, but nothing they seen was out the ordinary for a young man my age. I was always the quiet one growing up, and I never was a big talker, so they always just thought things were going well for me, they never seen the other life I was living. Little did they know I had already started selling weed in the neighborhood and in my school. Since I smoked weed myself, I already knew a lot of people that were always looking to buy some, so I started putting the word out that I was the man to come see. To distinguish my weed from all of the other guys who sold it, I would get a different type of baggie that was easy to recognize so people would know mine from everyone else. I also made my bags much larger than the other dealers as well. I knew this would reduce my profits in the beginning, but I knew I had to do something to make more people buy from me as opposed to finding someone else since so many people sold weed in the neighborhood. This strategy worked very well because I started selling out much quicker, and that allowed me to start buying larger quantities. I started working my job at Jewel and that allowed me to add some of that money to my weed business, which in turn allowed me to start buying even more. The guy who was supplying me started seeing me buy more and more from him, and at that point I found out he didn't have as much as I thought he did. It got to a point where I was looking to buy more than he could supply me, so it was now time for me to find another connect to supply me.

I ended up contacting one of my family members who I knew kept a lot of weed, lots of weight. He was big time, and I actually looked up to him because even though he sold drugs, he was a real family man and hosted a lot of family events. As a kid I loved going over his house to hang with my cousins, and he always showed me love. Since we had a pretty good relationship, I figured I would call him up and come over for a meeting to discuss this. When I first reached out he was very hesitant getting involved with me, especially since our family was so close. I explained to him what I already had been doing, and that I was actually doing pretty well. I emphasized that he could trust me, and that I pretty much so grew up learning from his actions, so he had nothing to worry about. After us talking a few times he agreed to supply me, but he stressed the fact that if I got caught, then I always would have to hold my own, because you never tell on others to get yourself out of trouble that you knew you were involved in. I told him I agreed completely, and he had nothing to worry about. That was the start of me taking my business to the next level. I now had a connect that could not only get me more weed, but also at a better price. I was so excited that day, my friends and I celebrated by drinking, smoking, and hanging out on the block-pretty much so what we always did when we weren't either in school or working. Business for me really started to pick up, and with the new connect supplying me in addition to my job, I was making more money than I ever seen before. It started to become a challenge hiding all of the weed and money since I was still living with my parents. I was able to save some money and purchase me a car, so I started hiding everything in there when my parents were home. When they were gone, I would hide it in the garage or a spot I had inside the house. My mom would always be on my back because I would start coming home late more often, and always smelling like weed when I did come in. She would not be on me that hard though because of the job. I would say I was working late, and since the Jewel I was at stayed open 24hrs, she would usually believe me. "Stop coming home smelling like that dope", she would always say. I would give her a hug and kiss and she would usually leave me alone. Me being the youngest it was hard for her to stay mad at me, so I usually took advantage of that. That was the type of person I had been gradually turning more into at that time, being very manipulative with not only women, but also my friends and the people I dealt with in the streets. I always told myself that I would take advantage of a person before they got the chance to take advantage of me. Being in the streets and dealing with the people I did, you had to always be a step ahead and never let anyone see any weakness in you, so I started to always keep my guard up when dealing with people, and I would never really open up to people either.

The more I was in the streets, and the more money that started coming in, I started to develop a real disrespect for authority figures, and it started creating problems not only with my parents, teachers, coaches, but also the local police. With my making what I thought was great money at the time, I felt no one could tell me anything, and I started being very cocky in the way I presented myself. It got to the point in school where my mom was getting called more by the principal because of my behavior in school. My football coaches, even though they seen I had talent and was a valuable member to the team, they even got to the point where they were tired of my attitude and was ready to release me from the football team. As much as I tried to be tough and blow it off like I didn't care, I really loved playing football and that actually hurt me, so I told myself that I had to change so I did not blow that opportunity because I was actually pretty good. With my oldest brother getting in a lot of trouble in our neighborhood, the police were already very familiar with our family, so me starting to get their attention was no surprise. They knew I was selling drugs, and they always would pull me over looking to bust me, but grew very frustrated because they could never find anything. By this time I had upgraded my first "hooptie"-as we called my first car, and now I had a nicer car that the police were very familiar with. In my new car I had built a "stash spot" where I could hide not only the drugs I would ride with to make deliveries, but also the gun I started carrying. I started seeing the jealousy from the other local guys start to grow as I grew my business, so I got the gun to protect myself. I mean, I had gotten to the point where some of the older guys who used to supply me, they were now buying from me and I was their supplier, and with that sent some mixed emotions. Some of them loved seeing me do well, I was still like their little brother and they were proud of my growth. You then had the other guys that hated that I was younger and I was doing better than they were, so I had to keep an extra eye out for them.

When I got to my junior year in high school, I was living some of the best years of my life. I still had my job at Jewel, which actually did not slow down my business as people started meeting me up there to buy weed from me, and this is while I was still on the clock. I was making more money-selling weed, but I would not quit my job because that kept people from asking where I was getting my money. At this point my friends had gotten involved in my business, so when I was not in the area I would leave them drugs and give them a cut off what they sold. This way I was not only making money, but also my team was making money with me. We all had more money, so we started hanging out more, buying more clothes and shoes, drinking more expensive liquor, and just having a good time. For a couple of 16-17 year old young men, we did not have a care in the world. At this time I also had a great system set up in school where I would keep my drugs in the lockers of the girls that I was messing with, so I never had to worry about getting busted in school. The school started getting wind of me selling, so security would always do random searches on my locker to try and bust me, but never could catch me with anything. Between outsmarting the police and now the people at my school, I felt like I could not be touched, and that increased my ego even more. I was very excited as I finished up my junior year because my oldest brother was getting ready to be released from prison, so I was ready for him to come home and see what his little brother had built. He already knew what was going on, and would always try to talk to me when I visited him or talked to him over the phone, but I would just blow it off as just "jail talk". Around this time I was the last child in my parents' house as my other brother had left to go off to school. This made my mom even more watchful over me as I was the only one left in the house, so I started getting frustrated dealing with that. My dad had pretty much so backed completely off of me as he seen me heading in the direction of my older brother and he just did not have the energy to deal with constant visits from the police, which started becoming more often, phone calls from school, etc. He felt like since I wanted to be grown then he would let me learn the hard way, he'd give me more tough love then my mom would.

Being the last child in the house really intensified the radar of my mother to the point where she became more of a private detective trying to figure out what I had going on. The neighborhood had already been talking about me selling drugs, so that was no longer a secret to my parents. The job being my front was slowly starting to fade, and the secret of me being a drug dealer was now out in the open with our community, my school, and also my family, so naturally this hurt my parents. Their youngest child with so much promise, the one that was good at sports, always very bright in school standing out from the other kids, now he was heading in the wrong direction of becoming another statistic. With my attitude at the time being the way it was, I really did not care what anyone thought, I was too focused on getting money and enjoying myself. If it did not deal with those two items then I was not trying to hear about it. Since my brother was downstate at school, I had started going down to not only visit, but also sell drugs with him. My brother had set up an operation of his own at his school, so when I came down to visit during the summer he would let me get money with him and his team. My best friend named Terry, who was more like a brother since we grew up together and our families were so close, he would come down with me as well and we would have so much fun partying with the college kids, and also make some good money while we were there. I looked up to my brother and his friends so much, and that made me work even harder to make my business successful because I loved the way they were living. They had all of the cute girls, lots of money, and were just enjoying life. Just visiting them at the college really opened my eyes up to the college life and I couldn't wait to go myself. We were all truly living our lives in the fast lane and did not have a worry in the world.

CHAPTER 4: LEGAL MONEY IS

TOO SLOW

As I finished up my junior year in high school and started my senior year, I was still working at the Jewel as a bagger and really started to lose my drive for the job. It seemed as if I would work so many hours and the paychecks really did not add up at the end of every week. The reality was the money I was making selling weed really made me start to lose my desire to even go into work since I was making so much more doing that. I started calling off work more, and when I did go into work, I would find a spot to hide out so I did not have to do anything. My attitude really changed, and I got to the point that I really wouldn't have minded at all if they fired me. I was in the union though, so it was pretty hard to get fired. There was a certain situation that took place that ultimately ended my employment with the company. There was another guy that worked with me who had approached me one day and told me that he had access to get a lot of weed at a very cheap price, even cheaper than what I was getting it for at the time. He was always talking big at work about all of the stuff he had, a real show off, so I figured he was just lying to impress me. I told him if he really did have it like that to bring a sample of what he had to work the next day we worked together and he said ok. He was a tall skinny kid from the suburbs, so I did not take him serious at all, I mean, in my mind I was this big time drug dealer from the city making all of this money, so I believed at time. I told myself that I could not take this guy seriously at all. The guy took me by surprise when he did actually bring the sample to work the next day, so I told him that I was interested in buying some from him. Little did he know, I never had any intentions on paying him, I talked it over with my friends and we decided that we were going to rob him for the weed. I played the role like I was going to pay him for it, but had no intentions at all to do so. This was my mindset at the time, I felt like I was untouchable and could do whatever I wanted without any consequence.

I discussed what I wanted to buy from him, and the guy ended up confessing that it was not him who had the weed, but it was actually a friend of his that had it. He was just going to pay him some money for setting everything up. I really did not care who had it; wasn't like I had any intentions to pay for it anyways. We ended up agreeing on a date, time, and location to do the exchange and set everything up. I wanted to make sure I was on my side of town, so I set everything up in my neighborhood. My friends were hesitant to even get involved with this, but I persuaded them into making this stupid decision, like I usually did, and they agreed to do it. We had my gun that I always carried with me, and then we had a BB gun that looked very real. We set up what we thought was this very detailed plan, and set everything in motion. In all actuality, the plan was very stupid, and we should have never even been involved with something like that. I mean, I tried my hand at being a stick up guy a couple of times, but my nerves were so bad on each occasion that I made the decision that it was not for me. This I felt was different though, a couple of naive kids from the suburbs, this would be a walk in the park I thought. The night came when it was time to make our move, and the whole evening was a disaster. My one friend got nervous during the stick up and did not come out like he was supposed to, the guys noticed something wasn't right and sped off, and the reality set in with them that I had indeed set them up. I now had to face the fact that I still worked with this guy, he knew I just tried to rob him, so what was going to happen when I went back to work the next day. Me being the big tough guy at the time, I felt like since they were from the suburbs they were weak and I did not have anything to worry about. I was wrong.

The next day when I went back to work, the guy actually did not come into work. This made me feel even tougher at the time because I figured he was too scared to face me and I assumed he quit working there. Such a punk I thought. About halfway into my shift, about 10 guys came into the store right as I was bagging up a customer's groceries. I was actually pretty nervous because so many guys outnumbered me, and I did not know what was about to take place. They all walked up towards me and started saying how they knew I tried to rob them, and how they had something waiting for me once I got off. I did my best to appear unfazed and unworried about anything they were talking about, but inside I was pretty nervous. Once I realized their whole point was to try to intimidate me, but had no plans of doing anything in the store in front of all of the people around, I started talking trash right back to them and there was a bit of a scene in the grocery store. The managers threatened to call the police on them and they ended up leaving the store. My manager immediately called me into the back and asked what was going on. I played like I had no clue, and that maybe they were just trying to bully me I told her. She was now worried about me, and told me to be careful. I ended up going outside and called my friends to tell them about these guys having the nerve to come up to my job and make that big scene. I told them to come up to my job with our gun just in case they came back to follow through on their threats. About 3 of my friends came up to my job immediately and waited around for the hour or so I had left on my shift. Once I got off there was no one around, so I figured they were just bluffing, trying to act tough, and I did not have anything to worry about. I told my guys to just go ahead back to the neighborhood and I would see them when I got there. They were very hesitant, but they ended up leaving since I had my gun in my car just in case. When I left work, I ran across the street to grab some food from the Burger King, then headed to the gas station, always watching my mirrors to see if I was being followed. Once I got to the gas station, I was about to run in and grab some cigars so I could smoke some weed with my friends, and as I opened the door I was immediately rushed on the driver side and the passenger side at the same time. I never even had time to see anyone coming, but all I felt were several punches coming from each side, and since I was in my car and caught off guard I did not have any time to react. I just pretty much so balled up and just took the punches until they backed off. As soon as they stopped I immediately reached under my seat and grabbed my gun, pulled the trigger back putting a bullet in the chamber. Right as I was about to start shooting I noticed the gas station attendant in the window on the phone frantically pointing my way. There were 3 guys in total and they all took off immediately once they seen the gun. Once I noticed the gas station attendant on the phone, calling what I figured was the police, I immediately put the gun away started chasing after the guys in my car.

I rammed the gas pedal and started my pursuit, in this quiet suburb where stuff like this hardly ever happened. I was livid! They had the nerve to jump me, and all I seen was red and I thought to myself, with my heart beating very rapidly, this would be my first time killing someone. The guys all split up when they took off, so I chose one and chased him out of the gas station and onto the next block where he ran.

My heart continued beating so fast. "This is it I thought, you have to kill this guy" I told myself. As I turned down the block chasing this guy, he immediately ran to some neighbors that were outside and started screaming, "he has a gun, he has a gun!! He's trying to kill me!!" The neighbors immediately grabbed their phone and called the police, and realizing this was a bad idea, I immediately turned around and sped off, promising myself that this definitely was not over. As I was driving back home I was steaming to say the least, and my heart was beating even faster at this point. I thought because of all the action I was sweating very profusely, and as I went to wipe my forehead I noticed my hand was covered in blood when I looked back down at it. As I looked in the mirror, blood was leaking from my head all down my face. Blood even got into my eyes as I was driving, and then I started to get dizzy. I drove over to a friend's house that was close by and told my friends to meet me over there. I tried to explain what happened, but with me being so angry I just told them to meet me and I would explain. When I pulled up on my friend's block there must have been a domestic disturbance next door to his place because there were several police cars on the block, along with an ambulance as well. My friends were already there when I pulled up and I jumped out of the car screaming, doing my best to explain what just happened. The police noticed all of the commotion then noticed me bleeding so badly, so they urged me to go with the ambulance to the hospital to get looked at. It turned out that one of the guys punching me had on brass knuckles and left me with several lesions around my head. I ended up having to get 32 staples in several spots on my head, and as they put each staple in my head the pain was excruciating, and with each staple I vowed that they were going to pay. That night the police came to visit me in the hospital; they placed me under arrest as I lay in the hospital bed, and they interrogated me about where I put the gun. The gas station had me on camera with the gun and showed them the footage. Me being a step ahead, thinking on my feet even in the midst of such a chaotic moment, I had my friends take the real gun out of my car and replace it with the BB gun we had. I figured if they decided to search my car that would explain the gun I had, which it did, and get them off my case. I was brought into the police station and questioned about the events that took place the next day. The police lieutenant was doing his best to interrogate me on how this all happened, letting me know that he was aware of the scene at my job previously. I refused to say anything to him, doing my best to appear as nonchalant as possible and tough as I could. After a couple of hours of getting nowhere with me he told me that I better not retaliate, and to let them handle things. In my mind, I was saying that this guy was insane if he thought I was going to let this slide, and the first opportunity that I got these guys were going to pay. I blew him off and told him that I had no intentions on doing anything retaliatory, but I said it in a way that clearly told him different. He told me that if I did in fact retaliate, that he would make sure they convicted me to the full extent of the law. I left out of that station that day blowing off everything he said, I was on a mission for payback from that day forward.

Due to the incident, I had taken a couple of days off from school. My head was bandaged up like a guy who was in a war, and I was actually kind of embarrassed to even go to school like that. I mean, I was supposed to be the big tough drug dealer, how did these weak kids from the suburbs catch me like this, at least that is what was going through my mind at the time. My older brother, who I love dearly to this day, drove over 6 hours from school that same night to come not only see how I was doing, but to come get whoever this was who did this to his little brother. That's the funny thing about us, as much as we would fight with each other growing up, there was never a situation that we did not have each other's back, and it's the same thing till this day. The second day I was off of school, one of my female friends at the time was ditching school to stay home with couple of my other friends and I. She wanted me to drop her back off around noon so she did not get into trouble with her parents. On the way home from dropping her off at the school, my friend and I was at a stop light when I noticed the guy who used to work with me a few cars up ahead at the light as well. I immediately put the car in park and was opening the door to jump out. My friend grabbed me and said that was not a good idea considering all of the people around us, he said let's follow him to see where he was going, so I stayed a few cars behind and followed him. He went to his house, which was right across the street from a elementary school, and at the time had several kids outside playing. We parked up the street and watched the guy go to his house. We crept into his backyard as he was entering his back door and caught him by extreme surprise, and from that point we started fighting him. In the midst of us punching and kicking him, I noticed a shovel close by and picked it up and started to hit this guy with it. It was as if I blacked out because I just kept hitting him with the shovel, all of my anger pouring out in that backyard. The memories of the guys jumping me in my car the other day constantly played over and over in my mind, and it only made me angrier. My friend noticed this and tackled me to the ground, telling me to get out of there before things really got out of hand. The guy lay on the ground bleeding very badly, screaming for help. We ran back to the car, and while we ran people across the street turned their attention to us as the guy ran up to the front screaming as he was bleeding, screaming for someone to call the police. As we drove off, my adrenaline pumping profusely, I felt like I got my revenge. The anger that I had from being jumped, the anger I had from the previous day of me being back at work, getting into a fight inside the store with a guy who made a joke about me being jumped and me getting fired, this all justified it to me. Little did I know the police would have my parents house surrounded, and that night the police would bust into their house to arrest me and charge me with assault and battery. My mother was crying, and hysterical, asking how could they arrest me and I was the one who got jumped, I was the one who had 32 staples in his head. Little did my parents know the events that happened earlier that day, and this would be my first serious case with the legal system. The lieutenant made sure he came to see me that day, and reminded me of what he told me. He called me a thug, and said that he better not ever catch me in their town again. With me still being young, not really having a background, in school, and working, I was able to get out of that situation with a slap on the wrist. I was sentenced to probation, and I had to complete several hours of community service. Both of which were a relief to not only me, but also my parents, who now officially knew I was selling drugs because I sat down with them and told them how the whole thing unfolded. My secret was out, and now my mother was on me even more, doing her best to prevent me from going down the same path as my brother.

I always loved learning and going to school. I mean, high school for me was 4 of the best years of my life. I was very popular due to me playing football, being the weed man, and just a real cool, laid back type of guy who messed around with a lot of females. I had turned into the guys I looked up to when I was younger, I was now one of them and I loved it. I was always very smart, and I was pretty much so finished with high school my junior year considering I had already accumulated enough credits to graduate then. There was two classes that the school required you to take your senior year, so aside from having to come my senior year to complete those, I really just came to school to sell weed and hang out with my friends since it would be my last year with a lot of them. That's when I even felt like going really, I would frequently ditch school and stay at home, usually persuading my friends to ditch with me so we could smoke weed and hang out. I had money to make in the neighborhood, so school started to really interfere with that at that point. I made good money in school, but not like being in the neighborhood. By this time I was moving much more product, supplying a lot of the older guys in the neighborhood, so going to school really was not my priority.

The more I sold weed in school, the more the school started trying to crack down on people selling drugs in the school. They started doing more "random" locker searches, but they were not very random at all. They had their eyes on a few people; me being one of them, so they would periodically even have the local police bring the K-9 unit to walk through the school as well. I was not worried at all because I never kept any drugs in my locker, nor in my own possession, I would use the girls who I messed around with and they would keep my drugs in their locker. Me being the selfish, egotistical person that I was, I really did not care about them getting caught, at that time all I really cared about was myself. I also had gotten pretty close to one of the school security guards, who actually bought weed from me himself, so he would always give me a heads up before they were going to do a search so I could make sure I did not get caught up. Things could not be any better for me, I felt as if I had all of the answers and could not be touched. The more the heat started to get closer to me, I finished up the required classes that I needed to take my senior year and made the decision to graduate a semester early. I mean, all I was really doing is hanging out, selling weed, and barely even going anyways, so I figured why even keep wasting my time going anymore. I was officially done with high school and ready to start the next phase of my life, and now that I would have more time on my hands, it was time really step things up in my drug business.

Even though I had finished high school and was not obligated to go to school at that point, I had decided to take a English course at the local community college with the goal of going full time once the next school year started. Even while I was enrolled in high school, I was taking courses that allowed me to earn college credits consecutively, so I had already accumulated credits at this particular college and wanted to continue doing so. At the time I had purchased a luxury car for myself to reward me for my success, a 1996 Oldsmobile Aurora, so I would ride up to my high school and drop my friends off to school a couple of times out the week. Since the college was out the same way as the high school, I figured I'd catch up with some old friends, but the ultimate objective was to show off and let everyone see how well I was doing. This further boosted my ego, as people would always come up to my car with amazement on their faces, just mesmerized with the life I had chosen. Even with the life I was living, I never wanted to stop going to school, and I always valued getting an education. At the end of the day, my goal was never to sell drugs forever, but my dream was to one day be a successful video game designer. With that particular career choice, I figured I could smoke weed most of the time, design and play video games, and life would be perfect. I enjoyed being in the college environment, and being around so many older women really kept me in attendance every time I was supposed to be there. I was young, but I was driving a nice car, nicer than most people's parents at the time, I had nice clothes and shoes, so I started attracting the attention of the older college women and that really kept me around the school more often. I also had noticed the opportunity to sell weed at this school, so it felt good expanding my business into a different environment.

As I was selling weed, I had a couple of accounts I used with a local bank in my neighborhood. There were a few branches in close proximity to my neighborhood, so this allowed me to spread out my deposits and never visit any one particular branch too often. I thought this would not draw too much attention to me since I was doing regular deposits with lots of low denomination bills. There was one particular branch I would visit more often than the others since there were several older attractive women that always flirted with me all the time when I came in to make my deposits. At the time I was unemployed from my last incident with the Jewel, so I needed to get another job to try and use it as a front for my drug business. On one particular day I came to make my deposit, the branch manager was flirting as usual, and she asked me why I was not in school since it was early in the day when I came in. I had told her that I had graduated early and was actually a college student now, saying it with so much pride, really trying to make myself appear older than I really was. She was impressed by this, and asked me if I wanted a job. The thought of working in a bank would be a great front I thought, it would stop people from asking me questions about my car and really make me appear legit. This particular branch was also about 5 minutes from my neighborhood, so I could still sell my drugs while I worked. I told her i would love the opportunity to work there, so she had me fill out an application right there and pretty much so told me that she would make sure I got hired. Working around beautiful older women all day, being able to sell my drugs without any interruption due to me being too far away from my neighborhood, and making some decent money, this definitely made my day to say the least. Within a couple of weeks I had been hired and had started my training at the bank. This was great news to my parents as well, because they could brag to their friends again about their youngest boy who was destined for greatness. I was only about 17-18 years old at the time, I had graduated from high school early and was enrolled in college, I had a good job at a bank, and they were very proud of me again. The recent incident with me getting in trouble was a distant memory now, and I was the shining star again.

I had been working at the bank for about 2 ½ months, and my business had actually been doing very well. When people wanted to buy weed from me while I was at work, I could just have them either meet me at the bank in one of the aisles of the grocery store, or I would just send them to one of my boys who also started selling weed. This allowed them to make more money as well, so things were good for all of us. I always looked out for my close friends because I did not want to be the only one making money; I wanted them to make some as well. As smart as I was, I was very dumb. I completely overlooked the fact that there were cameras all over the grocery store, and I am sure they were recording the majority of my sales I made. Me being young, dumb, and thinking I knew everything, I never thought twice about it though. One day when I was at work, I was on the teller line working when a gunman approached the teller next to me with a note demanding that he give him all of the money in his drawer. He also lifted his coat open slightly to show that he was holding a gun in his other hand. Out of the side of my eye I noticed something was going on, I guess it was just a gut feeling that turned my attention to him, and I noticed him holding the gun. Now, me being in the streets and definitely not trying to be any type of hero, I slowly closed my drawer and locked it, spinned around casually and walked into the bank vault in the back. From the vault I watched the teller give the gunman all of the money out of his drawer then take off out of the store. I was more stunned than anything because I was just about to call the bank robber up next to my station, but there was a pregnant woman that I knew and she asked him if she could go ahead of him and he let her, so he ended up at the station of my co-worker next to me. The event had caused such a stir in the branch because it was a majority of women that worked there with the exception of myself and one other guy (the one who got robbed), so the women were very shaken up. Me on the other hand, I was more amazed at the events that just had taken place. For a brief second I thought damn, that was pretty cool how he pulled that off, and he made off with a decent amount of money. The guy who robbed the bank had a bunch of bronze colored make up on his face that sort of had a reflection against the bank cameras, and it did not stand out because he looked as if he had been a burn victim and he was trying to cover it up with makeup. I did not look at him long enough to get a lot of details, so when the FBI came into the place asking questions I really could not provide them with much information. They seemed as if they had already stereotyped me when they came into the bank anyways, so I was on the defense as they questioned me. I was a young black male, with long braids, wore a very flashy watch, and I was working in a bank. In their mind I had to know something. I felt as if they were interrogating me way too much compared to everyone else, and they pretty much so insinuated that I had some type of involvement, which I definitely did not, so I started to get defensive and refused to cooperate. They told me they would be in touch if they had any questions, and in my mind later that day when I was thinking about it, I started to feel paranoid thinking they were now following me. The paranoia really started to stress me out, and I was very cautious moving forward. I had actually stopped making deliveries myself for a week or so following that event, making sure if the FBI was indeed watching me, I would make sure they only seen a young man who was going to school and working, nothing more than that.

A day after the robbery when I was working, I was counting my drawer down at the end of the night and my drawer counted an even $1,000 transaction "over", which is pretty much so the same as being "short". I was taken off the teller line while they investigated to see how this happened. While they investigated the transaction, they kept me off the teller line and I was assigned to walking throughout the grocery store asking the customers if they wanted to open an account with the bank. This was actually great news to me because I could now have all of my weed customers meet me at the grocery store again and I would meet them in different aisles of the store and make sales. I wouldn't appear so suspicious walking around the store all day, or at least I thought. After about a month of them investigating the transaction they never found it and they said that they had to let me go. The women working there had gotten pretty attached to me, so everyone was sad to see me go. After awhile I had missed hanging out with my friends, especially since it was time for stuff such as my senior prom, graduation, and all of the fun stuff that came along with that, so I really did not mind being let go. My oldest brother had been recently released from prison, so I figured I could use the break from work.

When I lost the job at the bank, my day started to consist of waking up, smoking weed and drinking with my older brother and friends, and riding around making deliveries. Now that my cover was gone with the job, now the police started watching me a lot closer, in addition to my mother watching even closer. She was actually worse than the police as she would constantly find some of my stash spots around the house, flush my drugs down the toilet, and constantly grill me about the large amounts of cash hidden in my car and around the house. Now that I had turned 18 years old, I felt like I was grown and it was time for me to start looking into my own place. My drug business was doing well, so I ended up blowing off the idea of going out of state to a Historically Black College (HBCU) like I always dreamed of doing. No, now I was just getting sucked into the life of a regular hood guy and my mother hated to see all of my potential just go down the drain, so yes, she stayed on my back every chance she got. I really hated it back then, but now that I am older I am thankful that she was because that prevented me from getting into some much worse situations than I did. She seen the path I was going in, and she even started advising my older brother to stop hanging with me so much in fear that I would drag him back down the wrong path. She knew my older brother loved me and would do whatever for me, and she did not want my lifestyle to influence him since he had been away from it for so long. There was one particular day my brother was in one of the local restaurants in our neighborhood getting some food, and he came across one of the old policeman that used to always get into it with him, but the guy was now retired. He told my brother that he heard that he was released, and that he heard around the station that he had been hanging with me and advised him against it if he wanted to stay out of trouble. He told my brother that my name was very popular around the station, and that they had my picture on the wall since they had me under investigation and were close to putting together charges to indict me. My brother played it cool and told him that he was not aware of what I had going on since he had just came home, but he would be sure to keep some distance. My brother immediately called me up so we could meet and discuss something important. When I met up with him he replayed to me the entire conversation that he had with the retired officer, and he expressed how worried he was about me. He did not want to see me have my parent's house raided, and he definitely did not want to see me go through the same situation that he did. I needed to get away from the area, and as much as I hated to leave the money I was making, I started making plans to leave. Around this same time a friend of mine had told me he was going off to a junior college about an hour away from the city, and they had recently built this new gated community where the students could live while attending the school. He explained that he was originally going with another friend, but he backed out at the last minute and it was now too expensive for him to afford on his own. I thought this was perfect timing considering the situation I was facing, so right then I made the decision to finally leave the nest and go off to school.

When I went off to school in Joliet, the apartment complex that I lived in was pretty much so its own isolated gated community full of college students. A lot of the students would throw parties on the weekends, so I actually liked staying in that environment. It reminded me of when I used to visit my brother off at school while I was in high school. We would go to school during the week, party from Friday until Sun, occasionally a day or two during the week, and this cycle repeated itself each week. With that being the case, I saw the opportunity to start marketing my weed business, especially since people always were looking for it. I was enrolled in the automotive technology program, so aside from weed, some of the guys in the program would also ask me if I knew where they could get cocaine and other drugs. I was never around cocaine while growing up; crack was popular in the area I grew up in, but never powder cocaine. It was more expensive, so it was usually more prevalent in areas that had more disposable income. A lot of the kids at this school came from those areas and were used to doing cocaine, much like in my neighborhood we were used to smoking weed. Just being in this new environment, I started to get exposed to lifestyles that I never knew existed growing up in my neighborhood. The kids I grew up around had parents who mostly worked blue-collar jobs, so there was a huge income disparity between some of the kids I was now living around. When people would ask me about the different drugs that they were doing I would constantly tell them that I had no knowledge of those, and I only sold weed. There were so many people that kept asking me about cocaine that I finally started to look into it. I reached out to a couple of people that I knew back home to get an idea of prices and how that business actually worked. There was a big difference in the price people purchased cocaine for back home compared to what people were used to paying for it where I was. They paid almost triple the amount that I could get it for back home, and at that point I knew it was time to expand my business. This was the start of my cocaine business.

Once I started selling cocaine the word spread very quickly, and I started to get more people coming to me making purchases. I was making money so much faster than I was selling weed, but it got to a point where I needed to get some help to not only keep up with the demand, but to also take me off the front line and keep me a low profile. I had already set up guys in two other apartments aside from mine to sell the weed at the apartment complex, I had a couple of guys back home selling for me, so I was still nervous because I did not know if the police were still watching me or not. The cocaine business carried much stiffer penalties if I got caught, so I had to be more inconspicuous in running that operation. I met a guy in my automotive program that used to always buy weed from me, and he would also buy cocaine to resale to some other people he knew around his neighborhood where he grew up. He kept telling me that the cocaine he got from me was so much better than the stuff people sold around his house, and he wanted to know if I could start supplying him because there was the potential to make a lot of money. When he said that he definitely had my attention, and after us sitting down and discussing how things would work, my new cocaine partnership was formed.

Around this time I had my first child Ashanti. I had come to learn that the girl Shelly I was messing around with back home was 8mos pregnant and she had kept it from me for the fear of me having her get an abortion. She came to visit me at my new place and I remember seeing her stomach looking so big, almost as if she was ready to have the baby right then. Now I was not very excited about her having a baby because I had stopped messing around with her, but with me having both my parents growing up, and having a good father in my life, I knew the importance of a man taking care of his responsibilities and I told her I would be there for her and my soon to be daughter. Knowing I had a baby on the way made me get more serious about making money, and at the same time it had me focus more on my studies because I did not plan on selling drugs forever. I figured I could have a good run while I was in school, then once I graduated I could have a nice nest egg as I started working in my career as an automotive technician in a dealership, then opening my own auto shop one day since I loved cars so much. I had planned everything out, and even though I would now have a family to think about much earlier than I had hoped for, I still figured things would work themselves out.

At the end of the school year, the majority of the people in my complex were preparing to pack up and go back home for the summer. The night before I was set to leave, I went back home and got my dad's plumbing van to move my stuff back home in. My roommate and I had the majority of our stuff packed in the van, and there were only some last items remaining that we had to pack up before we would head out the next day. Since this was the last day that my friends and I were going to be there, we had a party in our apartment. We were drinking a lot, smoking a lot of weed, and just having a good time. At some point the party moved down to the parking lot and some of the other residents had started complaining to the onsite manager about the noise. When the manager came over to tell us to shut things down, some of my friends and I started screaming and cursing at him, telling him we would shut it down when we were ready. Some of the residential assistants came down to help the manager deal with us, and at some point a big brawl and ensued. There was so much chaos, and fighting going on throughout the complex. People had started breaking windows and other property around the complex, and after awhile it seemed like every local police was on the scene trying to get the situation under control. They sprayed us with pepper spray, and several of us was placed under arrest and hauled to the police station. During the chaos, someone told the police that I threatened them with a gun, so they went to search my apartment. I was now nervous because even though I had gotten rid of the majority of my drugs, I still had some miscellaneous paraphernalia in the apartment, in addition to one of my safes. When the police searched my apartment they found everything and now in addition to being charged with inciting a riot and other charges, I was now facing drug possession charges and distribution. Things were going so well and I had one night before I was set to leave, and in a matter of hours things turned from bad to worse.

My brothers heard about this from my roommate; so they immediately came down to see what was going on. After I bonded out of jail that night, I learned that the police had impounded my dad's work van, I was now facing several charges, and I had to go back home to my parents house with all of this to deal with. Since I had been living away from my parents over the last year, I knew I had to find my own place, and quickly. At that point my daughter had been born, so her mother and I decided to get an apartment together. I would travel back and forth to court to fight the charges I was dealing with back in the town I caught the case in near my school, while now going to summer school at the college I started at right out of high school. I also kept my cocaine partnership going to keep some income coming in since I had to pay for the lawyer fighting my case. I was also working with an older friend of mine who had an automotive business working on cars. I had told myself that I would slow down on selling drugs after all of the stuff that happened, but I was having a hard time trying to support my family with the money I was making working on cars. This was the point where my partner who was selling the cocaine for me had gotten caught and disappeared, so that money was gone as well and things really got tight financially for me. That was pretty much my main pipeline to move the cocaine since I was not in the town anymore, so that had a huge impact on my business. I was doing my best to do things the legit way, but it was very stressful. I would constantly have migraine headaches, I was drinking more, and I just felt like I was at a very hopeless point in my life. I went from partying, making good money selling drugs, to trying to support a family off a few bucks every week, being a broke college student going to school at night, and just trying my best to hang in there until I finished up school and started my career making some good money.

Around this time I had gotten accepted into the Daimler Chrysler apprenticeship program at the college I was attending and they placed me in a dealership as an intern. I would now start making a steady paycheck every week, which was not much, but it was much better then the few bucks I would make working with my friend in his shop. Even though I appreciated him letting me work with him during that time, I told him that I would not be able to work with him anymore, as I would be starting my new position and working more hours. I felt this was a sign that better days were coming for me, so I had vowed that I would stop selling drugs completely and put my focus on entirely on finishing up school and doing well in my new job. As the months passed with me working in the dealership, the reality was that things were much harder being legit than I thought. I ended up having my second daughter Ariyannah with another female Danielle, exactly 6 months following the birth of my firstborn, so I really needed more money as there were now two little girls who needed me to support them. This is the point when my old partner popped back up with the proposition to make one last run that would make me some good money. This was the point when he had used me as his get out of jail free had. This was the point of betrayal on not only his part, but also mine. This is the point when I had let my friends down who looked up to me, them finding out that I had actually been selling drugs the whole time I was telling them to go to school like me, and work a legit job like I was doing. I felt like such a fraud talking with them. This is the point where I was set up with an undercover police officer and arrested for trafficking drugs. Now I had to face the more serious situation in front of me. Now I would find out what being greedy would get me.

CHAPTER 5: THIS IS WHAT

GREED GETS YOU

Before I could even turn to see what was going on, the door was snatched open by a guy in all black wearing a ski mask, and I immediately thought I had been set up and I was being robbed. It was as if time itself had just frozen and so many thoughts just started racing through my mind. Am I going to get killed right here in the crowded parking lot with all of these people to witness it? What about my baby girls, did I see them for the last time this morning? Damn I should've turned around. So many thoughts were going so fast, and my heart was beating even faster. As I was snatched out the car, I was immediately thrown on the ground, my face pressed into the pavement. All I could feel was someone with his or her knee in my back, hand behind my head, and I could barely move. I could not stop thinking about my family. I could not believe my life was about to end right here, right now in this rich suburb parking lot. It wasn't until I was able to slightly lift my head and see a marked police car that I finally relaxed. I was being arrested. I was set up.

As I was being put into handcuffs, I started hearing so many sirens, and all I could hear was the sound of cars revving their motors, racing around the parking lot towards me, with their brakes screeching to a halt. When I was pulled up from the ground, there were police everywhere, and there were men in all black wearing masks, some carrying large semi automatic weapons, others with pistols out- all surrounding me. All I could think of was damn, all of this for me? There were so many police and undercover officers on the scene it was unbelievable. People in the surrounding area were so scared. I could only imagine what they were thinking, all of this chaos going on in what they believed to be their safe, expensive suburb. As I was being put in the police car, my heart felt so heavy, my mind overwhelmed with fear. In addition to these feelings, I was very angry. I was angry with myself. I was angry with the guy who I knew set me up now. I always had my thoughts in the back of my mind, but this day verified it, so I was now angry with him. My mind was overwhelmed with the thoughts of what was going to happen to me next. I honestly believed my life, as I knew it was over.

Once I was booked into the police station, I was brought into the interrogation room. At this point I really didn't want to talk to anyone. After about an hour of different police coming in and out of the interrogation room, asking me questions, getting frustrated that I would not say a word other than me telling them I wanted to call my attorney, they finally left me alone. I was always taught that if you get caught doing what you know is wrong, you never "snitch" on someone to get yourself out of trouble. You knew what you were getting yourself into, you knew that it was wrong, it was illegal, and so if you get caught then you take your own weight. I knew I was in a situation that I had to do just that. They told me they were shipping me out to the Dupage County Jail. It seemed like only moments later that I was being loaded into another squad car and taking what seemed to be the longest drive ever. As we drove through this community I could not stop thinking about how amazing the homes were that we were passing. Multi-million dollar homes sitting up on tree-lined hills, homes I've only seen on TV in my lifetime. The more homes we passed, the more I knew this was such a bad situation I was in.

After I was processed into the county jail, I was told that I would get a bail hearing in the morning, and they told me to get comfortable because I was not going anywhere anytime soon. This being my first time ever actually going to the county jail, the fear of the unknown made me so nervous. Was this going to be like the movies? I did not know what to expect except the worst possible environment ever. As I was brought to the deck I would be on, all eyes were on me. It was like everyone stopped what they were doing and watched every step I took. I walked past everyone and headed to the cell that I was assigned to. As I was walking past everyone I couldn't stop thinking that this didn't look as bad as I thought. People were playing cards, chess, watching TV, even doing workouts in small groups. I started thinking that maybe this wasn't going to be as bad as I made it out to be. When I put my things in my cell I immediately went to the payphones to try to make a call. I was informed that the phones were off for the day and wouldn't be back on until the next morning. With all of the excitement I had for the day I was experiencing another one of my migraine headaches, and went to my cell to lie down. I guess with me being so young, and looking even younger, the curiosity of people wondering what I could've done must have been on their mind because people continued coming by my cell to ask what I did. I would be very brief, and very direct telling them simply it was a drug case. I knew I couldn't show any signs of weakness if I was going to make it in there, so I wanted to just keep my interactions with everyone to a minimum. I could not stop thinking about everything that went down that day, and most importantly I knew my family was worried about me. Back at the police station the police had confiscated both of my cell phones, and I could just hear them ringing off the hook. My best friend Terry and my girlfriend Shelly both knew where I was going and they knew I should've been back by now. I seen one of the officers answer my phone when my friend called and he tried to pretend as if he was me. My friend Terry, also knowing how this game went didn't fall for it, so they gave me the phone. I told him I was booked so he already knew what to do from there. As I laid in this yellow jumpsuit, lying on this slab of metal, I could not stop thinking about how worried my family must have been right then hearing this news. I knew this would be a long night, and that night I could not sleep at all.

The next morning I was brought to my bond hearing and they informed me that I was being held on a $200,000 bond, so that meant I needed $20,000 to go home. The hearing took place with me being in a room with a TV screen, so I was not able to see anything or anyone in the courtroom. Right then as I sat in front of the judge, listening to what now was my fate, my heart sank to the bottom of my body and right then I thought I would be held here forever. I was hauled back to the cellblock that I was being held at and I immediately went to the pay phone to make some calls. I knew I had to get out of this place as soon as I could, but I also knew $20,000 was a lot of money. How would I even coordinate putting that together? The majority of the money I had was used to buy all of the drugs for this deal, and now that was definitely gone. My first call was to my parents. Little did I know my mom, girlfriend, and some of my other friends and family all attended the bond hearing. They already knew the situation was very serious, and knew what I needed to do to at least bond out so I could go home. My mom told me to not worry, just focus on being safe and she would figure something out to get me back home. The Lord only knows how much I love my mother.

My sister had a contact that knew a very good lawyer that used to work for the Dupage County Prosecutors Office, and they did emphasize that he would be expensive, but he got results so I needed him. He came up to see me and we discussed our strategy to get me out of this jail. He informed me that the situation was very serious, and the whole time I'm thinking, "tell me something I don't know". He explained that his first goal was to try and get the bond reduced as much as possible so we could put the money together to get me out of there. The next day I had another hearing where they formally told me my charges and asked me how I wished to plead. I was charged with delivery of a controlled substance, which was a Class Super X felony, and it carried 9-45 years of prison time. As I listened to the judge speak, those words just kept playing over and over in my mind, and I was unable to even comprehend anything else she said after that. The feeling of fear overtook me and I could barely speak. My mind completely blanked out and it was as if my body was there, but my mind was floating in the air with several thoughts racing back and forth. While I was out mentally, my attorney was able to get my bond reduced down to $100,000, so now it would be $10,000 to go home. I guess this was my first "victory", that's if it could even be thought of as that.

When I got back to my cellblock I immediately went straight to the phone-as it seemed I did pretty much so everyday all day. From the entire time I walked back onto the deck, it was like everyone was aware of my case for some reason. You'd be surprised at how fast news gets around in jail. There was such admiration from the other guys on the cellblock; this young guy is some sort of drug kingpin they thought, which couldn't be further from the truth. Everyone wanted to talk to me, ask me questions, but all I wanted to do was get to the phone to see how

I was going to get $10,000 together so I could get home. I spoke with my mom and she said she was working on it, but it didn't look too promising. I felt so hopeless. Sitting in this jail, not being able to do anything for myself, this was the worst feeling ever I thought. The reality of me being in there was now settling in my mind, and it was a feeling that could not even be described with words. After the 4th day of sitting in the county jail, now I started talking with a couple of older guys that I had formed a bit of a rapport with. They kept telling me to keep my head up, and kept encouraging me that things were going to work out in my favor. With the charge being so serious though, they told me to keep in mind that I may be in here for a while. I mean, the charge carried 9-45 years, so at the bare minimum I would be looking at 9 years. That thought alone stressed me out even more, the hopelessness really started to settle into my mind. I called my mom earlier that morning to see how things were going, and she told me again that it did not look good at all. Sadly I told her ok, and that I had to go. I really didn't want to interact with anyone at that point. It was like the bad news in my life continued to flow in. Later that same afternoon my name was called over the intercom, "Cummings, pack your shit, you have been bonded out." Telling you that I was excited is an understatement; I could've won the lottery and probably not been as excited as I was that afternoon! The whole time my mom was telling me it was hopeless, that it didn't look very promising, little did I know they were getting the funds together, with it being so much money they just needed a couple of days to make it happen. My parents ended up taking out some of the equity in their home to get the money for this. I honestly did not deserve that from them at all. This was my mom's way of making me suffer; this was her way of letting the reality of my bad choices really sink in. I would deal with all of that later though; at that moment nothing else mattered. It was time to go home and get out of this place!

While I was in the county jail, my family called the owner of the dealership to let him and my manager know I had a family emergency and wouldn't be in to work for a few days or more. During the short time I was employed there I had made an impact on not only the owner, but also some of my co-workers, so they were concerned about me. Now that I was out I gave them a call and would discuss that with them when I came back in the next day or so. When we finally discussed it I told them everything that had taken place, and to be honest, they were very understanding. The owner especially was sincerely concerned for me, and I will never forget him telling me that whatever happened with the case that he would always have a job for me. He got to see my character along with my work ethic he explained, and he said he knew that wasn't really me, he knew I had a lot of potential and a bad decision should not ruin the rest of my life. I had the same conversation with my professor who ran the apprenticeship program that I was enrolled in as well. It was the same thing with him, I was very honest and told him what really took place. Believe it or not, the guy started to actually tear up because as he told me I had so much potential. I was doing so well in the program, better then a lot of the other students, and this he said was so hard to believe. You see, that was a character trait I've had all of my life, I was never the person to divulge a lot of my personal business with everyone, I was very quiet and secretive, so it was very hard to tell what I could be up to. The simple fact that these older white men, who probably could never relate to the life I was living, had been so sympathetic to what I was going through, so concerned about my future, that right there made me feel so bad because they truly had faith in me, and now I had let them down. Those conversations had me in tears as I talked to each of them, and I really felt terrible. As much as my professor really didn't know the extent of what I was facing, he looked me right in the eyes and told me to never give up, and he told me that however this situation I was going through played out, to make sure I come back and complete my degree. Words couldn't express how I felt knowing that as much as this situation beat me down emotionally and mentally, there were still people that had faith in me, and that gave me hope. That made such an impact on me, and I will never forget that or them.

While I continued working, I was going to court each month to do my best to come out of this situation with the best possible outcome. On my first court case while I was free, my discovery hearing, the state produced their evidence that they had built against me. The whole time I was dealing with this guy, they now confirmed what I pretty much so figured out in that he was an undercover tactical officer of their drug enforcement squad. Each time I delivered drugs to him, they had a video surveillance camera in the distance recording my every move. What also was very interesting to me, the officer wore a big gold chain, in in the middle of the medallion was what looked like a red ruby. That ruby was another camera that recorded each one of our interactions with each other, so they had several of those tapes as well. The state also produced another large envelope with several audiotapes in it. I would find out that these were wiretaps of both my phone lines. With these, they would listen to all of my conversations that I had on each of the phones. Needless to say, they pretty much so had me dead wrong, and my attorney would inform me that there was no way to beat the case, no loopholes that we could explore, so the reality was that I was going to prison, something within the 9- 45 year term that the charge carried. That reality, along with the seriousness of the case, really settled in within me, and the fear of what awaited me scared the hell out of me.

After that court hearing, my life started to get very stressful. I mean, facing 9-45 years in prison can do that to you, especially with me being so young. I started drinking more everyday after work, started smoking more weed to deal with the stress, and my life really lost the balance it seemed to have before. I would literally go to work, put on a facade in front of everyone like everything was fine, even knowing that pretty much so everyone there knew my situation, and just do my best not to think about everything else going on in my life while I was on the clock. As I mentioned before, I was very good at putting on a different face. Seeing me around the dealership you wouldn't even be able to tell I was dealing with this very serious situation. Talking to me you would think everything in the life of this 20 year old was just fine. Boy were they mistaken. I was so scared of what was to come, but being me I could never let anyone see this fear. I had to be strong, had to continue moving forward because honestly I didn't feel I deserved the right to sit and cry over this. I made a terrible decision that was going to not only forever affect my life, my future, but it was going to affect my family as well, and that thought alone just stressed me out so much more. It was like I was drinking and smoking weed just so I did not have to even think about it.

The next court date brought even more bad news, and as much as I thought the situation couldn't get any worse, here came my attorney with news that really brought me down to such a low mental state, I cringe even now with the same feeling I had back then just thinking about it. My attorney informed me that the state had offered me 15 years of prison time if I pled guilty to the charge they had before me. It was as if my throat sank into the pit of my stomach, I couldn't even deliver a verbal response to what he just told me. "15 years in prison" I heard him keep saying over and over in my mind, and at this point my life felt so hopeless. "How would I possibly get through 15 years in prison," I kept asking myself. This was my first time ever even getting charged with a felony, I was blown away at the thought of this even being for real. In the back of my mind I was just waiting for my attorney to tell me that he was just kidding, that he was just joking so I could lighten up. I mean, this definitely was not the time for jokes, but I definitely would not have been mad at all if it was. The reality was that it was not a joke, this was very serious and there was nothing funny about it. I just kept thinking, I'm only 20 years old; I would be 35 when I got out. My life was over I kept thinking.

My attorney explained to me my options. Thinking back on it, I can honestly respect how direct and straightforward my attorney was throughout the case. He never tried to "sell" me on anything other than the facts, and what was really going on. He told me that with the overwhelming amount of evidence that they had on me, going to trial was not even an option. If I went to trial and lost, which most likely I would, then they would really make me pay. He explained that me being a young black male in this rich suburb, selling drugs, which that reason alone would make the state's attorney make an example out of me-hence the serious charges I was brought up on. He told me that they heard me having phone conversations with the person I was getting the drugs from, and they wanted him. They didn't have enough evidence to pursue him, so if I agreed to set him up so they could get a conviction, then I would pretty much so have all of this not really go away entirely, but simply face a couple years of probation and never see the inside of a prison. My attorney explained to me that was pretty much so what happened with the guy I used to work with, and I was pretty much so the guy he had to set up to avoid him going to prison. Needless to say he had no problem in doing that considering my then current situation. My attorney explained to me that I didn't have to make a decision right then, but I had to let him know something by the next court date which was in a month. He explained that he was familiar with the hesitancy of people in my situation to "snitch" on other people, but his advice was to give this person up, whoever he may be, and get back to my life. He told me that from what he learned about me at that point, he could tell that I had a promising future and his advice to me as his client was to take this deal and move on. I drove home that day with a lot to think about. I was not a snitch. Never was, and I never would be I told myself. The same street terms that I was taught growing up prepared me for this exact situation, but as I continued driving home and thinking, I started to question it. I knew several people who snitched and came right back home, the people in the neighborhood knew it, but nothing happened. Then there were those other people who snitched, those people who were killed and their life ended. What in the world was I going to do I thought. I had a very big decision to make.

As the next couple of weeks passed, the drinking and smoking increased, I started gaining so much weight because of all the drinking and late night junk food. The way I seen it, I was about to go to prison for the next 15 years of my life, I might as well enjoy whatever time I had left as a free man. The way I was behaving, you would have thought I just received notice that I had only a few months to live, that I was going to die soon from some serious illness. Well, that was the way I seen it. My life was over. Once I went away to prison, everything I planned to do with my future was over I thought. Everything I was working towards was now over. This was what it all came down to in my life. My mind was already made up; I just couldn't bring myself to set someone up, especially this particular person because we were close. As much as this situation really sucked, I knew what I had gotten myself into and now I had to face the consequences of my actions. If I had to do 15 years in prison then so be it. The constant bad decisions I kept making in life finally caught up with me and now I had to deal with the consequenses. After a couple of weeks passing by, and the next court date approaching quickly, I informed my attorney that I would not be setting anyone up, and I would just have to deal with whatever came my way. He told me that he felt I was making a big mistake, but at the end of the day it was my decision. He never was in this type of situation in his life, so he could not relate to what I was going through. He told me that he would do his best to at least try to get the state to drop my charges down to a regular Class X felony, which carried 6-30 years of prison time, and with that he would try to get me the minimum of 6 years. Yeah, looking at it from both angles would still land me prison, but at least with that I wouldn't have to spend such a long time in there. I told him I appreciated it, and to please do the best he could.

On the next court date, my attorney had his motion to have my charges reduced met with a firm NO. The state informed us that they would not reduce the charges. They would make sure I learned my lesson because this type of activity was not welcomed at all in their county. They emphasized to my attorney what he and I already knew, that they had more than enough evidence to get a conviction should I go to trial, and if I did make the decision to go to trial, then they would aim to get the maximum number of years of prison time from the judge. Needless to say going to trial would not be an option. Since my attorney used to work for the state many years ago as a public defender, he knew the state's attorney and he got her to agree to offering me the minimum number of years for my charge which was 9 years. He informed me that in his opinion I should take it considering our limited number of options, so I accepted my fate and agreed. I told my attorney to just give me as much time as he could so I could prepare for this. He was able to get me a 2-month extension, and after that time period I would have to turn myself in to begin serving my time. At that point the situation really got up close and personal with me, and I now knew my exact fate. The feeling of hopelessness hit me like a ton of bricks.

During the 2 months I was out on bond, I would formally give notice to my employer and thank him for everything. He reiterated that he wanted me to keep in touch, and when I got through this situation I would have a job waiting for me. It might not be the same job, but he would make something happen for me. I explained to him how grateful I was, and that I would keep in touch. Since this all happened around the time the semester was ending at school, I was able to take my finals and complete my current courses on a satisfactory basis. My professor and I sat down and we both literally cried together as I sat there explaining what was next for me. He told me to please be strong, and to never give up. He told me to keep in touch, and to always know that starting back up in school would always be available to me. I thanked him and told him how much I appreciated everything he had done for me. I think the two of those conversations were some of the hardest out of everything I had to deal with because those were people I had only recently met in life, but they had so much faith in me. They did a lot to assist me within the apprenticeship, they believed in me, and I just felt like I really let them down. I felt terrible inside to say the least.

I had to now deal with my family. Even though my oldest baby girl was only a 1 year old, it was as if she picked up on the vibes that had been in the air since this situation had occurred. There had been several nights I just held her in my arms and cried knowing I would be away from her for so long. Knowing I would miss such a large portion of not only her life, but the life of my other daughter as well. Just looking into her eyes I knew I had to be strong for her and her sister. Even though they both were so very young, I knew I had to start being much stronger so I could make it back home to them some day. The idea to just go on the run crossed my mind more than a few times. Where would I go though I thought? How would I deal with the fact that I would lose the bond money my parents put up? Funny part is that my mom was all for me considering going on the run. "Maybe we can send you down south with our family where they can't find you," she would say. I still laugh today thinking about it, but this is why I love my mom so much. Good or bad she always had my back. Her loyalty and support for me during this time was indescribable. I was not going to run though. When the time came I would be strong and face what awaited me.

The time quickly came for me to turn myself in. It seemed as if that time had flown by so fast, but at this point I was mentally prepared to take this journey. My oldest brother had just been released from serving about 8 years in federal prison; ironically he was released about a year and a half before I caught this case. You can imagine the pain my family had to be feeling going through this process all over again, now with the youngest son/sibling. My parents felt terrible to say the least, and they were probably even more stressed than I was thinking of how their youngest son would survive 9 years in prison. My brother tried to explain to me that prison wasn't as bad as I was thinking, and that it wasn't like the movies and TV shows I had seen before. He knew how I handled myself in the streets, in life, so he emphasized to me that I could knock this out and come home a better man from it. Now I always looked up to both of my big brothers, both being a big reason why I chose the path I did, so him reassuring me of this had me relax some. I mean, he did all of those years and here he was just fine-he must know what he's talking about I thought. As my family and some close friends piled into different cars, all heading towards the courthouse where I would formally be taken into custody, I realized how much support I really had. I realized that I wouldn't have to go through this alone, and that maybe, just maybe, I would be able to make it through this and make a comeback in life.

Sitting in the lobby outside the courtroom with my family and friends, there seemed to be an overload of emotions. There were so many tears shed that day that it was such a challenge for me to keep it together. There was an overwhelming amount of emotions within me, but at this point I told myself there was not any time for me to sit here crying. It took everything within me to keep it together. It took everything within me to stay strong and not sit there and cry right along with the rest of them. I mean, in front of me awaited 9 long years in prison and I had every right to cry, but I didn't. I brought this on myself and it was time for me to deal with it whether I liked it or not. My attorney came out and told us that it was time, my case had been called and I needed to enter the courtroom. Damn I thought, the time is finally here. I didn't know what awaited me after that day, but then, right then, I put my chin up, stood up straight, and I walked into that courtroom and approached the bench of the judge that held my future in her hands. Behind me I could hear the screams of my kids, the deep heartfelt sobs coming from my friends and family. What hurt me the most though, was turning around to see my mother's face covered with tears, and her face bright red. My mother's anguish almost broke me down completely. The feeling I had right then almost made me lose this facade that I was so good at putting on. As the emotions built up within me, I turned around and continued what felt like the longest walk ever to stand in front of the judge.

As I stood in front of the judge, she reiterated my charges; she asked if I understood the charges and the terms I was presented with. "Yes, I do," I responded. As soon as I finished my sentence, out of the corner of my eye I noticed 3 of the sheriffs in the courtroom make their way towards me, and they formed a small circle around me, making sure I didn't try to make some last minute escape out of the courtroom. "Do you have anything you would like to say to the court?" she asked me. With as much pride and strength I had left in me, I responded, "No, I have nothing to say to this court." Her next words almost made me lose my balance, and fall completely over right there in front of her. My heart started racing with what seemed like a million beats per minute. "Here it comes, this is it," I thought to myself. "Larmon Cummings Jr., you are hereby sentenced to serve 9 years in the Illinois Department of

Corrections. Bailiff please escort Mr. Cummings out of the courtroom," she said. Right at that moment all you could hear was sobs and loud cries coming from behind me and I did my best not to even look back. I walked with my escorts as fast as I could to the holding cell in the back. As I made my way back there all I could think of was how did I get to this point in my life? There I was heading off to prison, and now it was time for me to adapt to a life I have never experienced before.

CHAPTER 6: LIFE IN PRISON

In the state of Illinois when you are sentenced, before you go to your designated prison they send you to a receiving institution where you are classified and they determine your security level to ensure that you are being sent to an appropriate facility that fits your particular charges. With me coming from Chicago, prisoners from Northern Illinois are sent to Statesville Prison, a maximum-security facility that houses some of societies worst individuals. When you first arrive here you are bunched into what looks like a huge dog cage, and you are stuffed in there with several hundred people all waiting to get processed in, and this is a very slow, stressful, and tedious process. You can just look in the faces of some of the people there and tell they were new to this environment, the look of terror written all over their faces. You could also tell the people who have been in this situation before, as they were very relaxed, joking and holding conversations with people they obviously knew already from going through the situation numerous times. When I was finally processed in with my group, I was taken through one of the most humiliating situations that I think I have ever faced in my life. "Strip down naked, open your mouth, arms up, bend over, cough, hold up your nuts", the correctional officers all screamed with what seemed like complete unison. Talk about feeling degraded. I did not feel like a man at that instance, did not feel like a father, a family man, no, I felt very low at that moment. At that point I just wondered how much worse of a situation did I have to look forward to. Feeling dejected, I was guided to the area where I received my extra large yellow Department Of Corrections jumpsuit, which was twice my size. I then received a brown bag, which contained my essentials, such as a small bar of soap, toothbrush the size of my pinky finger, and a tube of toothpaste that matched in size. From that point I was led to my housing block, and as I entered the area all you heard was screams, people banging on the cell doors, cursing at the officers as we walked by, and pretty much so complete chaos. This was what I had to look forward to.

As I waited in my new cell, with nothing at all to read, and nothing at all to do but listen to the chaos in the cellblock around me, it was like I just started to really reflect on what got me here in this situation. I felt so disappointed in myself, so ashamed. I could not shake the thought of being back in the courtroom getting sentenced, watching my mom and other family, friends, crying out for me. So sad at the point my life had come to. Constantly hearing the words from the judge, "Mr. Cummings you are a drug dealer." At that moment, the excitement of that lifestyle was not so glamorous. The folks I was looking up to growing up were not so cool right now, but now it was too late for me. At that moment I had 9yrs of prison time ahead of me, just waiting to make me yet another statistic like so many other young black men that came from my neighborhood. I had no choice but to deal with it. As I listened to the sound of grown men cracking up, literally going insane mentally trying to cope with the situation we were all in, some much worse than others, I made the promise to myself that I was going to be strong, that I was going to make it through this so I could get back home to my family. Just as I was having this mental revelation within myself, I heard some activity coming towards my cell. "Chow Time", the correctional officer screamed out. As they got to my cell, the face of the officer looked very familiar to me. "Hey, what's up bro, you remember me?" the guy called out. As I stepped closer to get a better look, it was a guy that went to school with me at the junior college. He used to always buy weed from me when I was there. He remembered the last episode at the school and must have figured I was in there as a result of that. No I told him, I caught another case and was sentenced to 9yrs. The look on his face was complete disappointment, and he felt very bad for me being here in this situation. He told me that I didn't belong there, and he told me to keep my head up, that I would make it through this because he knew I was strong. He gave me about 5 extra trays of food, and told me he'd come back later to chat it up with me. I took one look at the food and completely had no appetite at all. I would wait it out to see if something better on the menu came up, but that definitely never happened.

After about a week of staying in this maximum-security facility, stuck in the same cell 24 hours each day, getting the opportunity to come out of my cell only to visit the doctor for examinations, I really started to get mentally fatigued. How long would I be in this place? Is this what I had to look forward to for the next several years of my life? The mental strength that I had coming in was slowly eroding away, and I honestly did not know how much more I could take sitting in there. The environment was constantly filled with chaos 24hrs each day, with the noise never sleeping. My family had mailed me reading materials, money, and letters to help get me through, but I was told that I would not get access to any of that until I was transferred to the institution I was eventually going to be assigned to. I went several days of not eating, staring at the cold grey cinder blocks, with nothing to occupy my time. I was able to get ahold of a small flexible rubber pen when I took a trip to the doctor one day, so I started writing poems on the toilet tissue to not only occupy my time, doing my best to keep my sanity, but to also vent the frustrations I had in my head as I was going through the situation. It becomes very challenging to sit in a small isolated room for 24hrs a day with nothing at all to occupy your time. The mind starts to wander, and some of the places it wanders to can be very depressing, and can really kill any type of hope you may have, so I knew I had to get out of this situation and to my next destination as quickly as possible. I can only say God recognized this because after about a week, I was finally being transferred. The funny part about that is I was the same person who started to think like an atheist, saying there was no God. Now here I was praying fervently for God to please save me from this situation, give me the mental strength to just hang in there. As much as He should have turned His back on me like I did Him, I was informed that I was now on my way to Vandalia Correctional Facility, now I was on my way to experience the next phase of this journey.

As the bus pulled us into the prison and stopped to unload us, we were taken to the intake section of the facility. Several white officers were lined up and screamed for us to line up in pairs, walk in a straight line, and shut up. You could tell from the vibe in the air that I was not in Chicago anymore, no, this was southern Illinois and I would learn that things were much different down here compared to being back home. As we were walking to the building one of the officers behind me screamed, "Shut up nigger, before I really give you something to talk about!" "Did he just say nigger", I thought to myself, completely taken aback. This is the year 2010, no, I had to have mistaken that one. Another black guy who I sat by for the ride down and was talking to confirmed it when he looked at me, and the look on his face said it all. Once we got into the building to get our clothing, the next shocker hit. They were issuing us used underwear, used socks, along with used uniforms! "Did they seriously expect us to wear this stuff," I thought to myself? Some of the socks had holes in them, the underwear had stains from the previous owner, and some of the uniforms were torn and totally worn out. The clothing room consisted of majority Hispanic inmate workers, so they actually gave the guys that they knew all new clothing items, and from seeing that I knew I had to figure out how I could purchase my own new clothing because it was no way I would be wearing that stuff.

During the time I was in the first facility, I was unable to use the phones or get visits, so my family really didn't know what was going on with me at point. I was anxious to get a phone call so that I could update them on what was going on. With me having a non-violent drug offense, I was classified with a lower security badge and was sent to this place, which was a Level 7 minimum-security prison. They did not have cells, but had large dormitories that housed about 100 inmates. It was a large open room with rows of bunk beds neatly arranged in long organized rows that stretched from the front of the building to the back, with the showers and toilets to the rear. I would later find out that was where all of the fights took place because it was out of sight of the guards, who were usually sitting in the front of the building at a desk. There was a gate that separated the inmates from the front where the guards were, so you would have to get buzzed in to get back to your bunk. As soon as you entered the place there was cigarette smoke everywhere, which I truly hated, and it was almost as if the air was grey. It seemed as if everyone was just chain smoking back to back, only taking a break to roll up another one to smoke. That smell combined with the odor of bodies not bathing for probably several days, along with grown men passing gas freely into the air, so I was immediately disgusted and sick to my stomach. I just kept thinking to myself that its better than the place I just left, so I had to put my personal preferences aside and deal with it. I was no longer a free man, no, I was now considered inmate #R50712 and I didn't get to complain about the living conditions not being up to my standards.

Once I was showed to my bunk, I immediately asked the guy who was now my neighbor, how did the phones work. He explained it to me and I went to make my first calls. I called my family and told them that I was fine, where I was at, and to send money fast so that I could purchase my necessities. They told me that it would be on its way the next morning, and that they would be down to see me as soon as I let them know they were approved on my visiting list. That first night was filled with people talking quietly because there was a rule that after 9pm no talking was allowed, men passing gas, cigarette smoke constantly funneling through the air, and I just thought to myself that I would never get a good nights rest for some time. The next morning around 5am a loud siren went off to alert us that it was time for breakfast. From not eating much the last several days I was starving, so I definitely was not going to miss that. Once I got there I came to see that I definitely wouldn't have missed much anyways because the food looked as if someone just slopped a pile of rubbery oatmeal on a plastic tray, along with a boiled egg, and a juice box. Yeah, I couldn't wait until my money arrived so that I could go to the commissary to purchase my own food along with other items, so I knew I would just have to hang in there until then.

The next couple of days went by with me pretty much so keeping to myself, rarely talking much to others because I was still adjusting to the reality of being in the place. I still did not receive the money my family sent, but then one day I guess all of the stuff they sent to the first place finally caught up with me, so I now had some letters, books, and a few hundred dollars. I was very excited because I would be able to purchase the items that I needed so I could start establishing some sort of comfortability. There were several inmates who heard what I was in for and figured I would have some money coming soon, so they would always offer me food and other items, insisting there were no strings attached and they were just being nice. Me being from the streets I knew people were not just nice people, so I respectfully declined, telling them I would be all right soon. Some took offense to it, which I really did not care at the time, and others who probably did just want to look out for me told me that if I changed my mind then it would be there waiting for me. Being in this place for the few days I was there, I took the time to really evaluate my surroundings, taking note of the different people who I was now forced to cohabitate with. I noticed the shady hustlers, the bullies, the guys who got taken advantage of, the different gangs, the laid back guys, and I just kept a mental track record of who to stay away from and who I could actually see myself socializing with. I kept telling myself that I was not in here to make friends, no, I was in there to do my time and get back to life as I knew it. The counselor came to visit our dorm to discuss a few things with some people. He gave me my calculation sheet that showed me my projected outdate for when I was scheduled to be released. We were just into mid-March of 2006 and since I had bonded out and really had no time in, my mandatory projected out date stated February 18, 2015, which would be the release date if I served all 9 years. It then it stated a date of July 18, 2010, which was my sentence at 50% and me getting 6 months of good time if I stayed out of trouble. The counselor explained to me that under normal circumstances I would be able to earn more good time if I went to school, but since I was charged with a Super X felony, I was not eligible for any additional good time. He also explained that the same thing applied to work release, I would have to wait at least 24 months until I could even apply for that, so the reality was that I was not going anywhere anytime soon.

With me not having any violent felony cases in my background, I was eligible to go to the work camp, which granted you more freedom and privileges, at least that is what they explained to me. When I was sent to the work camp I had purchased a lot of the things I needed to start getting settled in, but I was still not settled in mentally. The work camp did provide a more relaxed environment, so the change was appreciated. There were smaller living areas, instead of all 100 inmates in one big dorm; they consolidated it down to 5 rooms with only 20 people in each of them. Since the kitchen was not cooking for as many people, the food was slightly better, but still nothing to get excited over. You were able to get access to better clothing, and I was now able to enroll in some college courses. If you were going to be at the work camp you were allowed 2 options, you either worked a job or you went to school. That decision was a very easy one for me, not only because I liked going to school, but I definitely did not have any plans to get worked for 8 hours each day to make $30 a month. The work campers cut the grass in the community, shoveled the snow, among a variety of other tasks, and paying them $30 per month seemed very close to modern day slavery to me and I wanted no part of it. Over the years I began reading more and learning how true this was, but I will come back to that later in this story. The local community college offered college level courses along with vocational courses in the prison, so this allowed the inmates to not only get their GED if they didn't have it already, but also pick up trade skills along with college credits that they could use on the outside once released. I had started taking an automotive vocational course for my 8 hours each day in the mornings, and then I signed up for two college courses offered in the evenings. The goal was to not only keep myself busy learning, but to also stay out of the dorms with the rest of the inmates as much as I could. There was so much negative energy back in the door, so I wanted to just distance myself from that as much as I was able to. The inmates that attended school for the most part had a desire to pick up some useful skills for their release. There was also a lot of inmates earning good time that would send them home earlier than planned, some there for the sole purpose of staying out of the dorm as well, but overall we all pretty much so wanted to stay out of trouble so we could get back home to whatever it is we all were going to. The simple fact that I was able to go to school really helped me in the coping process in dealing with the situation I was going through.

The college offered a variety of college level courses in the evenings, but the ones that caught my attention the most were the psychology courses. These courses helped me really get a better understanding of the choices I made growing up, and I learned a lot about not only myself and why I behaved the way I did, but also I learned about the human behavior as a whole. Going to school really helped pass the time, and that was a big part of being in prison. Deciding how you would spend each day while incarcerated was crucial to how you ultimately would fare once you were released. There were people that spent the majority of their day by way of gambling playing cards, some people worked as much as they could to pass the time, some sat around or slept the days away, but at the end of the day we all had 24 hours and everyone chose which way they wanted to spend them. Being around a lot of men that went to prison frequently started to become very annoying to me, not because they went to prison multiple times, no, it was more so the fact that they refused to take things seriously. It was a way of life to a lot of guys in the place, so finding people who could hold meaningful conversations, or expecting the older men to have wisdom to pass along was such a rarity. Yes, a lot of the decisions these guys made to land them in here repeatedly was nothing more then their fault, but seeing such a disproportionate number of minorities, especially black and Hispanic men, made me start to look at the situation much differently. A lot of these guys came to prison when they were very young like I was, and once released opportunities for them to change did not exist. When your neighborhood refuses to give you job opportunities, no matter if you have an education or not, it leaves few options for a grown man to pursue in order to survive. A lot of these guys come home and go back to doing the same things that landed them in prison, not because they just enjoy doing them, no, its because they really don't have any other options, especially considering the men who need to provide for their families. The more I seen this, I vowed to myself that I would not stay a statistic as I was at that time, no, I would work my butt off to be different.

Since I could not be in school my entire day, and there was no school on the weekends, I began doing a lot of reading and also hitting the gym a lot. I started reading urban novels and they really sparked my interest in reading again. I would sometimes read entire books in a day or so, being so intrigued with the story lines that I felt as if I was watching a movie. A lot of the books had story lines similar to what got me in prison in the first place. Stories about selling drugs, living life in the streets, so these novels took me out of prison mentally and brought me back home with my people. I would be so engaged in the books, reading them so fast that I was constantly having my friends and family send me more. I had enough money on my books and the majority of the items a person could want in prison, so the main thing I asked for when my family or friends asked what I needed was books. At this point in my journey I had been away for several months. Both of my kids moms would come to visit about once or twice consistently each month, then my friend from high school Crystal would come each month. My family would come every couple of months as well. We only were allowed 5 visits each month, and I used every last one each month; I was very homesick and missed my family. The guards started to wonder whom this young kid was who barely said much to anyone but a few, who was this guy that had visitors each week? I received lots of mail since I would constantly write my friends and family almost everyday. Little did they know I was loved by a lot of people, and I was not some kid without a strong support system. The regular visits and mail helped so much in getting me through this journey, and I always tried to express to everyone who did support me how much I really did appreciate it. Since I was not a big talker and wild like a lot of the younger guys my age, I connected more with the older guys rather than the younger guys around my age. People started trying to get closer to me asking more and more questions trying to figure out what was to me. I only chose to associate with a few people though, some good men who my instinct told me were safe to be around, and men that were about growth and development in their lives, not having this situation become a permanent and repetitive part of it. Just because I was in prison did not mean I was not the same guy at heart though. A lot of the guys who I was locked up with, these were not the type of guys I would even hang out with on the outside, so hanging around them constantly in prison just did not make sense to me. The older guys I hung around reminded me of my older brothers back home and they had a similar mentality of my friends I was with all the time on the outside, so I connected with them just like I did with the guys back in my neighborhood. Some were drug dealers from a variety of different neighborhoods who were about living life and making money, guys with families that may have just made some bad decisions, and we just had very similar backgrounds even though we came from very different areas. Yeah, they could tell I was much younger regarding my age, but they could tell my mental level was that of someone much older. They really looked out for me, I looked out for them, so these were sort of like my new older brothers away from my real brothers back home.

People complain a lot in prison, myself included, about the environment, the treatment from the staff, the food, you name it and there is someone complaining about it. That is the point of prison though, not to accommodate you into a comfortable, enjoyable environment, no, its supposed to be miserable to prevent people from wanting to return. Some of the treatment from the staff went much further beyond this though, the constant racist remarks towards the minority inmates, the excessive force, the harassment, the threats and intimidation, yeah, they did much more than was required or even allowed by law. Even with constant complaints and grievances from inmates regarding those staff members, they never seemed to have any impact in changing things. They take advantage of the people who do not have a voice, people who do not have a support system on the outside to help report the injustices that go on inside the prison system. People in similar situations as I was in, with lots of time ahead of them and the fear of being transferred to a higher security prison, a lot of the activity by the staff went unreported for fear of facing retaliatory actions in return. After being in Vandalia for over a year, I felt it was time to transfer to another institution to see if I could at least get into a more reasonable environment. I was starting to get into more trouble with the staff, and that was going to prevent me from getting out of this place if it continued. I was having a hard time adjusting to the racist attitudes of the staff, the harassment by the staff, and the more I spoke out against it, verbalizing my discontent, the harassment started to get worse with them claiming that I felt I was better than the others. It all came down to the fact that they did not like the fact that my family and friends consistently visited me every month, that I received mail from them everyday, and that I was not struggling to survive in this place as they felt I should as a young black man in prison. I was not letting myself become apart of this system and they did not like that. I refused to let the system consume me and turn me into someone who I did not want to become. My family started to go through more hassles when they came to visit me, at times driving the 5-6 hours to come see me only to be turned away because of various excuses made by the staff. I complained to the warden, but he would always say that it would get discussed with the staff and nothing ever changed. I put in a transfer to another facility called East Moline CC. The way some of the inmates described this place, you would think it was the Disney World of prisons! "You get ice cream on commissary!" one inmate said excitedly. "Man, you get to walk around outside all day, even have your own key to your cell!" another professed just as excited. "You get to buy your own TV and that helps make the time go by faster." another person chimed in. Yes, I can admit that there are certain items that seem very irrelevant to people on the outside, but to inmates doing time, these items can make the time much more bearable. With that being said, yes, the way they described the place and the different amenities that it had did make it attractive to me, but I honestly could careless about that stuff. Getting into this facility would put me so much closer to the city and my family, so they would not have to continually endure the long drive all the way down to the very racist southern town that I was currently in. I worried so much about them every time they visited me for the unknown fear of what could potentially happen to them. After waiting close to 10 months for my transfer approval, being in this town that I never even knew existed for almost 18 months, I was finally notified that my transfer had been approved. I was leaving this place and off to a place considered to be so much better, or so at least that is what I thought. I had no idea that this transfer would change this entire prison experience for me.

CHAPTER 7: SOLITARY CONFINEMENT

When I first arrived at East Moline, it almost looked like a college campus. There were several large buildings that sat on acres of land surrounded by trees. You seen inmates walking freely around, some sitting under trees reading, others playing basketball and other outdoor activities, and in my mind I thought maybe this would be a better environment after all. The setup in this place was different from the last prison as it had two man cells as opposed to the large dormitories. I think I was more excited about being able to have a cell and deal with only one other person instead of being in a large room filled with several people, chain-smoking cigarettes, and be able to have at least some level of privacy. When I first came into my assigned cell block, people were out hanging out, playing cards and watching TV, seemingly much more relaxed than the place I came from. So far what I had seen since I arrived appeared to be a lot better than the last place, and in my mind I felt like maybe being in this place would make the time go by not only much faster, but much more smoother. When I came to my cell, my cellmate was laying down on his bed with his feet kicked up watching TV, looking almost as if he were at home relaxing. My first thought was that I had to get my own TV as soon as possible, no matter what it was going to cost me. I pretty much so stopped even watching TV at the last place because they were controlled by the staff and was much to noisy to even hear what was on. I was reading so much I really didn't even think about the TV unless there was a football game on that I wanted to watch. We introduced ourselves, and I unloaded my things so I could start getting settled in. Since I transferred from another institution and had already been incarcerated close to 18 months at this point, I had all of my own property that I needed, and I had a good grasp of how things worked. I was no longer the new guy, but in a place mentally that told me this was my way of life for the next 4 years. I believe that is the point you get to when you can actually move on mentally and do your time, not stressing as much about what is going on the outside, worrying about what everyone else back home is doing. No, when you get to this point you understand that there is no going home, and you have to be strong enough to finish the time out so you can get back home. It's a challenging point to get to, but once you do it does remove some the mental stress you experience on a daily basis.

Talking with my cellmate, he excitedly showed me the large commissary menu full of items I had not seen since I was locked up, and he broke down the times our deck went to eat, and pretty much so how things operated at this place. I was excited about the new college courses offered here, the new schedule, and the new way of life that the place had to offer. I was now only about 2 hours from home, so my family would not have to travel so far to see me. Things were really starting to look on the up and up, I mean, given that I was still in prison, at least the environment appeared to look a little more bearable from what I was seeing. I seen they offered a culinary arts vocational program, and from what the other inmates told me, you got to eat a lot of different foods outside of what was offered, so I signed up for this program immediately. I was excited to be able to eat some new food, especially food outside of what I was used to seeing, so once they told me I would be starting the upcoming week that really gave me something to look forward to. Things continued to get better for me, and I started to really believe coming here was the right choice.

My first encounter with trouble came when my friend Crystal came to see me. Since I had been incarcerated we had grown much closer, and she consistently wrote me weekly, came to see me every month, and supported me in everyway she was able to. At this point both of my daughter's mothers had stopped coming down to visit, probably around month number 16 or so. I guess they both had found someone else while I was inside, so as much as I liked them coming to see me with my daughters, I figured it was probably best that they moved on with thier lives. They both were young and attractive, so I did not want them to put their life on hold waiting for me for the several years I would be incarcerated. I still had a lot going on in my personal life at the time trying to get through this challenging situation, still trying to figure out who I really wanted to build my future with, and with them I just did not see that happening long term because we all were changing. I found out they both had started looking for other people to be with, I was getting much closer to Crystal, so I took it everyone was satisfied and had moved on with their lives. I have to admit that I was sad not being able to see my kids on a regular basis anymore, and I missed a lot of their lives, but I knew I was not in a position to do much for them being locked up, so my focus was on bettering myself while away so I could be a better man, better father, for them when I came home. Since Crystal regularly visited me, she was used to the process that came along with being admitted into the prison for visits. For some reason there was a younger white female guard that had a very bad attitude who usually was in the visiting room, and really had it out for me with no justification whatsoever. One particular day when Crystal came to visit me, she said the top that she was wearing had a cut that was too low, so she either had to put on another shirt or she would not let her in. As I waited anxiously in my cell waiting for them to call me, as I always did on days I expected a visit, I began to wonder if something happened. I had gotten used to the constant harassment and issues that came along with my family coming to visit me, so I did not know what was the case this particular time. When I finally got called out, Crystal explained what they had put her through, and they only let her stay if she turned her shirt around backwards. I was livid to say the least. To make matters worse, the officer hovered over us the entire visit since there were only a couple of people in the visiting room, and she was constantly picking at everything she possibly could. After about an hour into the visit, the lady seen us holding hands, which is permitted on visits, and she told us the visit was over. Completely furious, I started demanding to see her superior because this was ridiculous. Crystal seeing the situation get out of hand, and not wanting to see me get into more trouble, told me she would just leave and to call her later. Doing my best to control my anger, I said my goodbye and reluctantly left. Saying I was angry is an understatement. I started to see maybe this place was not so great after all. Being away from my family like this, the only things I really cared about were my visits, my mail, and commissary. Other than that I really did not care much about anything else. Them messing with my visits was going to be a problem.

After my first year of being incarcerated, my parents had sent me a bible to start reading, and I had begun just reading the bible daily. There was a small publication that I found which was titled "Our Daily Bread", and I read that each morning and the associated scripture that related with the story for the day. Even though the bible seemed very challenging to understand, I started to discuss it with other men that I seen not only going to services regularly, but the men who I seen conducted themselves much differently daily, really applying the information they were learning. I wanted to get a better understanding of the bible, and with me wanting to change my life, I knew there were some things I needed to change spiritually. I read a book that really put it into perspective for me, and it said in order to live the life that I was looking for, I would have to actively build myself up mentally, physically, and also spiritually. I started praying individually on my own for the first time in my life, and I honestly started to feel a sense of relief and strength take over my body. I set a goal to read the entire bible from cover to cover over the next year. I knew if I was ever going to make it through this situation I would need help, and I knew the help from God would be the biggest. I knew I had some nerve as well though; me being the guy who used to say there was no God. Me being the guy always doing wrong, always going against the majority of the stuff being taught to me when I was younger. I was just glad to find out that God is much more forgiving than humans are, and knowing this gave me the assurance that I was going to make it through this situation. I made it my goal to rebuild my relationship with God, no matter how difficult it would be for me.

Over the time I was locked up, I started to get a much better idea of how the legal system worked-within the prison system and outside of it. I learned how to write grievances when injustices were done, and this really made a lot of the staff react in very retaliatory manners. Again, with me being a young black male caught up in this system, I was expected to be uneducated, wild, and unable to represent myself in a respectable manner. With me conducting myself in the total opposite manner, I was not liked much by a lot of the staff, and I faced a lot of harassment with that. My cell was searched more often, doing their best to destroy as much of my property in the process. I had to wait longer to get called for my visits, sometimes making me miss a lot of the time allotted for spending time with my family. My mail would get ripped up before being given to me, among a lot of other unfair treatments toward me. As much as it angered me, as much as the old me wanted to lash out, I was growing up, maturing more and more each year I was in this place. I started to develop more self-control, and I practiced holding my tongue in different situations to prevent getting myself into more trouble. With doing this, there began to be a lot of built up frustrations within me, and with me not having anyway to vent these frustrations, trouble was sure to find me at some point. I worked almost everyday in the gym and that helped release a lot of the stress, but there were days when things were very difficult to deal with. The crazy thing about it all was that I rarely, if ever, had any issues with the other inmates. The majority of my troubles came from staff interactions, and I know that was largely due to me having such a hard time taking orders from individuals who were naturally racist at heart, and a lot of their hatred towards me came simply from the fact that I was black and they viewed me as being beneath them. Not only that, but I carried myself much differently than how they expected me to act. They would constantly tell me that I felt I was better than everyone. I guess that was because I had a desire to go to school to learn new things. Maybe because I kept what they felt was a lot of money on my account. Maybe it was due to me having a subscription to USA Today newspaper, Money Magazine, and I started reading more business based literature. It may have been due to me slowly drifting away from reading the urban novels to more business oriented books, books about the stock market, real estate, books that would prepare me for my next phase of life once released. If that's what they felt made me think I was better than them then so be it. I made it a point to carry myself in a manner that told everyone that met me that prison was not my life, but the result of a smart young man making some very bad decisions along the way. Growing up in a neighborhood where I fell into the temptations that lured the majority of the men I was incarcerated with into the life of crime, but seeing that was not the life I wanted for myself and making the choice to change. If that made people upset then I did not care, I knew it would make this situation harder for me, but little did they know that each occurrence of injustice towards me made me work harder to better myself so I would never have to go through this experience ever again. I truly hated every aspect of it.

One day after school was out, I was back on the deck and everyone was either out hanging outside of their cell, or some were just in their cells relaxing. On this particular day, I had received a notice from my counselor informing me that I had been denied for work release, yet again, so the reality of sitting in here the entire 4 years slowly started to become my reality. Already feeling kind of stressed, I called my kids mother to check on my daughter. Hearing from my kids usually made my day much better, and hearing them start talking more and expressing that they actually missed me. I ended up getting my oldest daughters mother pregnant right before I went away, so I now had three little girls that I was missing precious moments with each day that passed. While we were on the phone, I was having a hard time hearing because the deck was usually so loud. With everyone out and about, the deck was normally very noisy with people all over the place, so with the phones being right in the middle of all the noise, it was usually a challenge to hear the other person on the phone speaking. As I was speaking to her, she told me that she had been seeing someone else, and since we had not been on good terms recently, I believe she was trying to hurt me. I don't know if the reality of her sleeping with someone else had hurt more, or the fact that she had clearly moved on with her life, but I can honestly say that it really upset me knowing I was stuck in this place and could not do anything about it. At this point our communication had been reduced dramatically since I was at the last facility, I rarely responded to her letters, and I did not want to get visits from her anymore. This was my way of trying to hurt her before, and it was really me just being frustrated with the whole situation I was in. I guess my feelings were hurt from our last conversation when she expressed wanting to explore the option of being with someone else, which considering my current situation I really had no right to be mad at her. By this time I had been gone close to 20 months, so I can admit that I was very hypocritical in my reaction considering I had never been faithful to anyone I've ever dated in my life, always cheating on whoever I may have been with at the time, messing around with numerous women since I was a young kid. Watching the older guys growing up I thought this was how you were supposed to be when it came to women and relationships, always having multiple options. I did not have the right at all to be mad in the least bit, but being incarcerated kind of does that to a man. You being far away from the people you love, not having any control over what they do or don't do, it does cause a lot of stress. You are completely powerless and totally dependent on the people on the outside, and for me being the self-sufficient type of person I was, this was another one of my harder parts to cope with during this entire experience. I was used to getting my own on my own terms, never depending on anyone for most of my life. With us on the phone having this conversation, me boiling with anger on the other end of the phone and completely oblivious to what was going on around me outside of the phone booth I was in, a hand reached into the phone booth and clicked the phone off. I immediately turned around to see who had the audacity to do something so stupid like this, and as soon as I turned around there was the officer monitoring the deck at the time standing right in my face. This is the point when this entire experience changed directions for me.

As the officer stood almost nose-to-nose with me, screaming with his terribly smelling breath, and spit flying out of his mouth into my face, my mind totally blacked out. Thoughts of me getting set up and betrayed, being sentenced by the judge, me sitting in the maximum security prison cell alone with nothing to do, the racist officers along the way, the constant harassment from staff along the way, the harassment my family faced when visiting me, and definitely the harassment I consistently faced from this very officer; they all flowed through my mind very rapidly over and over. I lost it. I spit in the officers face, screaming right back at him. Stepping right into his face and ready to fight right then and there. My fists balled up ready to destroy him in everyway possible. Now, with this being a minimum-security prison the majority of the inmates have an out date that is not very far away, so the staff takes advantage of this, and constantly tests you to try and make you choose that one bad decision to react and blow it all. This particular officer definitely fell into that category, consistently harassing inmates everyday he worked and he received constant complaints and grievances from inmates, and some of the other officers even expressed their dislike for him as well. He was the kind of person that would make you get yourself get into more serious trouble, and get kicked out of this place along with more time added to your out date. With everything going on, with all of the built up frustrations and stress within me, I lost control and reacted without thinking. I had gotten tired of the harassment though, gotten tired of biting my tongue and taking the nonsense that some of these officers brought to work with them everyday. On this day I lost it, and they would make me pay for it.

The officer was taken completely off guard by my reaction, and seeing that I outmatched him, he hit his panic button, started screaming into radio like I was attacking him, and he immediately ran off the deck. I never even put a hand on this guy, and standing there I knew things were about to get worse very quickly. I tried to run to my cell to gather some of my belongings because I knew what was coming, but as I went that way the riot team was on their way in to get me. With the officer calling in an officer in distress call; they came in with complete force. There was about seven officers total that I seen rush me; throw me onto the ground, me feeling punches in my back, my stomach, as they rammed my face into the concrete floor. I was unable to do anything with there being so many people, so I just closed my eyes and took the beating. As they hauled me off to solitary confinement, or "Segregation" as they called it, I could feel my face bleeding and swelling at the same time. Thoughts of me never coming home started playing through my mind, and immediately it was as if I started having a panic attack. My breathing started racing, my heart beating very rapidly, and my mind seemed like it was about to completely explode. The fear of what awaited me next stood at the forefront of my mind.

Sitting in the cell, alone, without any other property or reading material around immediately had me flashing back to when I was back in the maximum-security prison. I had no idea how long I would be in here, nor what was going to happen next. All I could think of was how upset my mom would be, and how devastating this would be to my little girls. All of the time I spent over the last 2 years trying to better myself, really make sincere changes to mature into a better man, all of that ruined in mere minutes. I was so furious at the guard, at myself, and sitting in this small cell, with no one to look at or talk to but myself, I laid down and tried to sleep the rest of the miserable day away, hoping the next day I would wake up and realize it was all a bad dream. I woke up sore the next day to someone banging on my cell door with breakfast, and all I could do is tell them that I was not interested. With everything going on, eating the slop that they had on the menu was the furthest from my mind. I wanted to talk with someone to figure out what exactly was going to happen. There was an older officer that worked the morning shift, so when he came past to do his rounds I asked him if he knew what they were charging me with. He said that he heard briefly what happened the previous day from the other officers, and they were supposed to be charging me with assault on a officer, which would land me a new case if I was convicted and definitely bring with it more time. That, in addition to a few other charges, really sucked the life out of me mentally and all I could do is just try to lie down. With all of the noise going on, sleep was not going to come easy. You see, in solitary confinement, the objective is to break a person mentally, and the longer a person stays in there then the more of an affect it will have on them. You could literally hear people breaking down mentally on so many levels, and being in the same environment with them almost sucks you in as well. The sounds of people banging their heads on the doors, sounds of people screaming out for help, it all adds to the objective to make a person feel as hopeless as possible. There was a young guy who tried to hang himself while I was in there, and luckily they caught him in time before he took his own life. There was another guy who would cut himself just to get taken to the hospital. People were just looking for a way to get out of the cell, if only for a couple of hours, because that could mean the difference between life and death in some situations. I can honestly say the first couple of days were very challenging to me mentally, but what awaited me would present a much bigger challenge.

After the first couple of days passed, they finally came to my cell to hear my tickets that held the charges against me. The lieutenant read the charges and asked me what happened. I replayed the entire situation, really explaining how things went down, not how the officer had painted the picture. The officers already knew the reputation of the guy making the accusations against me, so he luckily dismissed the assault charge and let me know that he really did not believe that based on my current behavior record so far since my incarceration. They did end up getting me with disobeying a direct order and disorderly conduct. Just hearing the charges made my heart sink into the pit of my stomach, and I wondered what would be the consequences from these charges. I was sentenced to 30 days in solitary confinement, my privileges were taken away for 30 days, and last but certainly not least, my security badge was raised and I would be given a disciplinary transfer into a higher security prison. As the officers walked away from my cell, I sat there in complete shock, wondering how things on this journey seemed to finally be coming around for me, and now took a completely different turn for the worse. The fear of not knowing where I would be getting transferred to really wore down on me mentally, and over the next few weeks stress really started to consume me. I did not have any desire to eat, so I lost lots of weight and my body did not resemble myself in the least bit. They finally started to give me my mail, and I can honestly say the letters from my mother, from Crystal, those are what really helped me keep it all together. After a couple of weeks I was granted a visit, so my dad had informed me that he would come to see me with my mom. I could not wait for that day to say the least.

The first, and only, visit I was granted in solitary confinement would be a memory forever stamped into my brain. When you are in solitary confinement, you are not able to have any physical interaction with the person(s) visiting you, and you have to sit behind a huge bulletproof glass and talk to the other parties via a pay phone. During this time, you are dressed in a bright yellow one-piece suit, and you are shackled up as if you are a mass murderer. Your hands are chained to a small box that connects to a chain that wraps around your waist, and that chain comes down to your ankles, where there are another set of cuffs around both ankles, with another small box connecting them. As I was escorted from my cell, I was only able to take small steps, and it was a challenge trying to keep my balance. As I entered the visiting room, escorted by 3 officers, it was if the entire visiting room turned their attention to me, all of their eyes wondering what in the world this young man could have possibly done to be in that situation. I saw one older woman raise her hand to her mouth in shock, almost looking as if she wanted to cry. I could just imagine how bad I looked. Constantly losing weight daily, my hair severely unkempt, definitely not the way I normally carried myself. The first site I had was of my dad sitting in a chair with my 7yr old nephew. The look on his face when he seen me almost made me break down right there. He immediately was afraid and I could see the tears start to come down his face as he gripped my dad's hand in complete fear of what stood in front of his eyes. I was a very close part of his life growing up, him being with me very often, and he was always used to seeing his uncle looking good, doing well for himself, but definitely not like this. Seeing me like that had to really scare him, especially since my parents had brought him to visit me several times before, but this time was much different. The officers escorted me to a small tree stump that they provided as my seat, and I looked at the sadness on my dad and nephews face as the guards proceeded to secure my chains to ensure that I would not go anywhere. It took several minutes for the rest of the room to take their attention off me and go back to visiting with their families, even still constantly turning around to look back my way. When I picked up the phone to speak, words so hard to even get out, I said hello and asked where my mom was since I was expecting to see her as well. My dad had informed me that she had not stopped crying since this incident took place; not really getting any sleep, worrying about what was going to happen to me. Just hearing my dad talk it took every ounce of strength in me to hold the tears back, trying to be strong and not show any weakness in front of my nephew who looked up to me so much. We talked for a while, my dad taking the time to pray for me while he was there, telling me to be strong, and it seemed like before I knew it my time was up. Just like that I was being hauled off back to my misery, and looking back at my dad and nephew, who started crying again as I left, I was praying in my mind that I just keep strong and make it through the challenging situation I was dealing with.

Sitting back in the small cell, with an even smaller window tucked away in the corner, it seemed as if the room started to shrink each day. I found myself talking to myself more, talking to the walls, just trying to cope with the situation and not lose my hope, not lose my sanity, but it was very challenging. I started to get insomnia due to the constant noise that never seemed to die down, so that caused me get frustrated and get severe migraine headaches, and it had me start to get angry with the people making the noise. The lighting in the cell was very dim, so reading started to become a challenge and it also caused frequent headaches due to me straining to read the words. As I sat in that small cell, I may have been losing my mind, but I truly believe that was the first time that I actually heard God speak to me. The words that He spoke to me reminded me of a scripture that I read before, and the scripture touched on the fact that God would never put you in a situation that you could not handle. That's not to say you won't have to deal with some very challenging situations, but with the strength that He gives all of us, we can overcome it and grow stronger and wiser from it. Sitting in that cell on that particular day, something came over me and I felt a sense of relaxation and calmness that I never felt before. In that instant, I knew things would get better and I would not only make it through this, but I would grow much stronger mentally from it. After sitting in solitary confinement over 45 long, challenging days, 15 days longer than I was even supposed to be in there, I was informed that I would be getting shipped out in a matter of hours to Western Illinois Correctional Center, also known as Mt. Sterling due to its location in the town with the same name. This is a level 2 high security prison, and with me having close to 2 years left on my sentence to serve and no hope of going home any earlier, I had to prepare myself mentally for the next phase of this journey.

CHAPTER 8: PRISON AIN'T NO JOKE!

When I first arrived at Mt. Sterling, sitting in the processing area with the other inmates, I was talking with a few of the other guys and there were a lot of people who had gotten in some type of trouble at their transferring facility, so they were being shipped here on disciplinary transfers as well. The common theme was that this particular facility housed a lot of troublesome offenders, so this started to have me kind of nervous. Here I was with close to 2 years left to serve on my sentence, and talking with some of the other inmates they had much longer sentences than I did. One guy 15yrs left to complete. Another guy had already been incarcerated 16yrs and still had another 17yrs to go. Here I was with what seemed like eternity to me, but hearing from some of the other inmates it made my situation not seem as bad as I initially thought. The nervousness started to settle as we were given the run-down of how things worked around this place, and I learned that we would be locked in our cells 21 hours out of the day, with a morning and evening dayroom access, or the choice of going to the gym/yard for recreation of about an hour. In addition to that, we could come out of the cells to eat the three meals provided daily, but outside of that there was no other movement outside of your cell. The only other option you had to get movement outside of your cell would be to take on a job assignment, or enroll into school. I think I was more excited about the schooling because they offered some different vocational programs and college courses at this facility, one of them being a business management program. I had started reading more and more books on things like real estate, business, the stock market, and other related concentrations, so them offering a course like this really appealed to me. There was an older Arab man I met in Vandalia CC that introduced me to the stock market, so since then I had been very intrigued with learning more about it, and I even picked out a couple of stocks that I monitored on a regular basis via my USA Today newspaper to simulate me having them in my own portfolio. To some, the idea of being in your cell for so many hours of the day was unbearable, but with me fresh out of solitary confinement, I had gotten comfortable being more isolated. I now had all of my property back, so it did not take long for me to get settled in. The experience being in the large dorms with so many people smoking, stinking, and making so much noise also assisted in me being more comfortable alone and not really socializing with too many people. I was escorted to my cell where I would meet my first cellmate in this higher security prison.

When I was first escorted to my cell, there were a couple of older guys who came up to me and casually asked what gang I was plugged with. They seen a couple of my tattoos and immediately asked if I needed anything, thinking I was just coming in and brand new to prison. I had lost so much weight, and my hair had grown out, making me look as if I was homeless I guess, so they wanted to see if I needed anything. Once I explained I had already been locked up almost 2 years already and had all of my property, they just told me that they were there if I needed anything. They ran down who had control of this particular deck, how things worked here, and just told me to stay away from trouble since I had such a short time left, at least compared to the majority of guys here. I told them thanks and went to my cell to make my bed, get settled in, and see whom I would now be living with.

As I was getting settled in, my cellmate came in and introduced himself. As we talked, he had informed me that he had been incarcerated for over 19yrs and still had another 12yrs to go. I guess with him being incarcerated for so long, he had a very laid back demeanor, similar to myself, and he picked my brain as to what was new going on in the world on the outside. With me only being 2yrs removed, we talked about new technology and a variety of other things. We ended up getting along pretty good, and once I was accepted into school I was moved to another unit where people going to school were housed. Once I started school and got a regular routine going again, I was able to not pay so much attention to the time passing and was able to just focus on each day at a time. I really liked the business management program I was taking because it opened my eyes up to wanting to continue studying business on a higher level once I was released. All of the books on business that I had been reading recently all sort of tied together with the concepts that I was now learning in the class. The program lasted about 10 months also, so that gave me a bit of a timeline to pass the time. As each month passed, I really focused on reading more and really trying to prep myself for my release which was quickly approaching now, and my outdate was more in my grasp as opposed to when I first started out. The more I talked with the men in my unit, the more I started to see the disproportionate sentencing that was imposed on a lot of minorities in comparison to other races. There were a lot of men that had been incarcerated since they were teenagers, and here they were now in their late 20's, 30's, and some even in their 40's and 50's. They had pretty much so spent their entire lives in the prison system, so for the men who were fortunate enough to be scheduled for release in the upcoming years, they had no clue as to what they were going to do once they left. The fear of not being able to adapt and become a productive member of society again hung over a lot of the men who resided with me in that place. For a moment it made me start thinking about the same things, wondering if I was unable to find employment now that I was a felon what else would I be able to do on the outside. During the period of time that I was incarcerated I seen countless men be released, only to show back up with new cases. Some I even seen come back more than 2-3 times, and I was still trying to get released from my same sentenced! I made a promise to myself and I vowed that no matter how hard things got, I would never do something to get myself put back in this situation ever again if I could prevent it. It caused too much pain not only for me, but it had severe consequences for my family as well.

Once I finished the business management course, the instructor had seen the type of person I was, not causing any trouble and really having a strong interest in business, so he asked if I wanted to take on the position of his teacher's aide position since the previous guy had been recently released. He seen that during the time I was taking classes there, I had made not only the college's President's List, but I had made the Dean's List as well, keeping straight A's for every course I had taken. He told me that with me trying to apply for another transfer to a lower security prison, it would be in my favor to get a recommendation from him, so I told him I would accept the position. It also would keep me in school, as they had informed me that they were no longer going to allow me to go to school anymore since I exhausted the maximum number of college courses allowed to be taken. I thought that was crazy, but I guess the state did not want to pay for too much education for any one particular inmate. I also liked having the time out of the cell, not lying around all day like so many other people around me. It helped keep me in a positive environment around some good guys, so I thanked him for considering me. I had also recently put in a transfer to get out of this place, as it was coming up on close to 18 months since I had been there. My family and friends would still come visit me, and Crystal and I had grown even closer. Our relationship had grown so strong over the years, and I promised her once I was released that we would get married and start a family together. I knew things were going to work out for me as long as I surrounded myself around good, positive people, and being around someone like her kept me with the right mind state. When I got back from visiting her one-day, I had gotten informed that I had finally been approved for my transfer. I was going to be transferred to Jacksonville Correctional Center, which would move me closer to my family, and it was also a lower security prison that would allow me to have more privileges and movement. With me being as close as only 6 months away from my release at that point, I was very excited about what was next for me. I just had to keep a low profile until I was shipped out and avoid any trouble in the meantime. There were several officers that did not like me and had been trying to find any reason to harass me, so I definitely had to avoid them as much as I could.

Being in a high security prison around people who on average had not only been incarcerated for several years of their lives, but who still had several years to go, the potential for violence was greatly increased. There were more staff assaults, people got stabbed over card games, and with me not too far away from my release date, I made sure to stay away from being around the wrong people. A lot of the violence came from the stresses of being incarcerated though. Being away from your family year after year, losing loved ones and not being able to be there to support your family, wives and girlfriends leaving you and you not being able to do anything about it, all of this created so much pent up frustration among the inmates who are incarcerated and it does not take much to just push someone over the edge. I watched a man get savagely beaten for unknowingly step on someone's foot and not say "excuse me". I sat steps away as a man was stabbed in the eye with a pencil for cheating while playing cards. I stepped out of the way just in time as a officer was beaten for not letting a guy make it to the yard line to go lift weights. All of these incidents always were followed by the entire institution being put on "lock down", in which you are locked in your cell 24hrs a day, sometimes for weeks at a time, only being let out once a week to take a shower. Unconscious to me, but this entire situation had slowly turned me into a much colder person, and my family and friends started to notice it. I stopped smiling, because no one smiles in this environment or it can be seen as a weakness. Violence stopped shocking me, and it just became a way of life that I did my best to avoid, but it was just something you keep on walking past if it did not concern you. Men would sit around and joke about shooting people, killing people, beating people, the same way people on the outside would converse about current events. This is was life was about in this type of environment, and for a lot of men it was all they knew. Living with people like this has the affect of having an influence on a person after awhile. I had been away so long that I even started to talk with a southern accent from being in southern IL for so long. The transition from solitary confinement to high security affected me a lot mentally, and I really questioned if I would ever be able to live a normal life again after this. I prayed constantly for God to just keep working on me, helping me to just stay strong enough to make it out of this situation because I had four little girls that needed their father. I did not want to come home and be a very distant and cold person towards them, but I wanted to be able to show them love like they deserved from their father. I knew the transition would not be easy, but with time I was confident I would be ok. One day after we had been on lockdown for going on two weeks, the officers told me to pack my stuff, and that I was being transferred.

Again I realized that God was truly with me, and the reassurance of me being just fine once I was released was confirmed.

When we first pulled into Jacksonville CC, it did not look as rural as the other prisons I had been housed at. I could actually see more homes and cars driving by, and not all of the cornfields like I had grown accustomed to seeing. It actually made me feel like I was closer to home, in an environment that I was more familiar with. At that point with me being so close to being released, close to 6 months left, going home was all I could think of. Leaving behind a lot of good men that unfortunately did not have a second chance at the prison I had just left, I was just grateful that I would have the opportunity to go back home with a lot of life left to live. When released I would be 25yrs old, so I knew I had to really get serious about preparing for my release. I had already started putting together some business plans for companies I was going to pursue starting once I was released. I drafted a business plan for a vending machine business, coin-operated laundromat, along with a real estate company. I also started researching the process involved with opening Subway franchises. With me being in the business management course, I was able to get access to books that showed me how to put together business plans, and in addition to that, I had my family send me books as well on the subject. I was determined to make the best out of my second chance in life, so I really started putting my vision down on paper so I could have all of my notes once I was released. It was like the more I got closer to my outdate, the more excited I became, but at the same time I was very nervous as well. I really did not know what awaited me once I was released. Now that I was a convicted felon, who also served a lengthy prison sentence, I wondered if I would even be able to find a job. I was incarcerated during the most recent economic recession and it was hard for people with college degrees and no background to get a job, so the likelihood I would find something seemed very challenging. Talking with the other inmates, most people expressed that while on parole you would usually need to find a job and I questioned if that would even be possible. The fear of being another man returning to prison and not making things work on the outside really hung above my head. I definitely did not want to be like the many guys I had seen return back to this miserable environment. I definitely needed to get those thoughts out of my mind, and what I needed to do was start praying more and attending the church services more often to rid myself of those negative thoughts.

When I got settled in to my new residence, I was assigned to work in the kitchen. At this point they no longer would allow me to attend college, so keeping busy with a job in the kitchen really did not bother me. I would come to find out there were benefits to working in the kitchen, you got to eat better food than the rest of the inmates, so I appreciated this considering I had been eating the same thing in a variety of ways over the last three and a half years of being locked up. It also made the time go by faster, so I definitely appreciated that. My schedule started to consist of me working in the kitchen, going to the gym, and staying pretty much so to myself and reading along with studying as much as I could. In this particular prison, there were a lot of men transitioning from being in higher security prisons serving very long sentences, to now being close to their release date and ready to go home. The sad part of a lot of those cases were that some of the men had been incarcerated so long that they did not have a home to go to. They did not have a family waiting on them to be released, so the fear of the unknown really scared these men. Some were going to homeless shelters, others just trying to really figure it out. This is where I looked at my situation and really realized how blessed I truly was. Over all of the years of me doing no good, here it was that God still stayed with me, keeping me with a very strong and committed support system, and to say I was thankful would be an understatement. I signed up for the religious service that was offered once a week, and there was a very positive group of men that attended the services each week. I really started getting along with a few of the older guys, who in hearing my story really encouraged me to do well once released, always telling me how there was just something different about me.

After a couple of months being housed on the main area of the prison, I was informed that my security badge was reduced again since I had not been getting into any trouble since my last incident, and since that had taken place I would be getting shipped to the lower security work camp. There was supposed to be more privileges and more freedom to move around, but since I had been incarcerated so long I did not really get too excited about this move. At this point, in my mind it was all prison and I was only concerned about counting down my last months in this place. The counselor did inform me that since my security badge was lowered, me being on the work camp with the amount of time I had left I would be a good candidate for work release. There was a part of me that wanted to be excited about the news, but the reality of what I had been through over the last few years of my life did not allow me to. I had been disappointed so much over the years, and at that point I taught myself to not get excited over anything unless it was finalized. Prison will do that to you though, it is meant to depress your happiness, suppress your optimism with constant disappointments and bad news; at least that is how I viewed it. The constant heartaches that I had endured over the years would not allow me to get excited anymore about anything anyone had to tell me and left my heart very cold. The only thing my mind was focused on was my outdate, getting home to my family and my life, and anything outside of that did not move me in the least bit. I was a man on a mission and I would not let the misery of the prison system toy with my emotions any longer. The clock was ticking and my only goal was to keep a low profile, and stay out of trouble until I was being led out of this depressing system that had changed my life forever. Whether I stayed where I was at, or moved to the work camp, either way I was going to finish strong and leave this place behind me forever, so when they came to transport me to the work camp I said my goodbyes and never looked back.

Being at the Clayton County Work Camp was not too much different than the Vandalia Work Camp, much less racism, but still prison to say the least. I was assigned to the kitchen again, and at this point I actually had gotten used to eating some different foods, much better than what everyone else had to eat. There were some good guys that I worked with, so passing the time became easier. I had gotten into a routine and was ready to knock out my remaining 4 months when I had received a letter from the counselor informing me that I had been approved for work release! I could not believe what I had in front of me, so I immediately requested to see the counselor, who informed me that what I was reading was in fact true. I was going home! After over 36 months of my life in this nightmare, I was finally going to be free, well, partially free. Even though I would be in the work release center, I would be able to go out and look for a job, see my family outside of the walls that contained me for so long of my life, and I had to just sit down and let it all sink in. Without even realizing it a tear started to fall from my eye, and the last few years of my life quickly replayed in my mind. That was all going to be behind me now, the next chapter in my life would begin soon. I was not the same immature kid that came in here before, no, now I was a mature man ready to get out and handle my business. With all of that, I closed my eyes and silently prayed to God, thanking Him for everything, also asking him to prepare me for what was next to come.

CHAPTER 9: LIFE ON THE OUTSIDE

Before reaching the work release center, inmates who are heading north towards Chicago have to transfer back to Statesville Correctional Center; I was praying it was not the part of the prison I was in initially. Since I was headed to work release, I was not housed in the maximum-security unit but in a minimum-security part of the prison where I would wait until a bed opened up at the work release center. This came as a surprise as I was under the impression that I was going directly to the work release center, but I figured waiting a few days wouldn't be that bad at all. With me being so close to my freedom, I just took the time to continue preparing myself for life back on the outside. I continued going over my business plans that I had created. I continued reading through my books and notes I had compiled over the years. I was determined to overcome the fear of being free again that consumed so many men that come through the prison system. After waiting for close to 2 weeks at this facility, I was informed that I was being transferred to the work release facility the next morning. Things finally started to seem more realistic, all I had to do was make it through the rest of that day and I was heading out the next morning. The excitement did not allow me to sleep that night, as I tossed and turned throughout the night, trying to imagine how things would be at the work release center. I would soon find out things at the work release center were not as good as the other inmates made them seem.

The ride to the work release center was in a regular van as opposed to the big windowless prison buses that I had grown accustomed to traveling in over the years. It felt so good to just be able to take a ride, minus all of the shackles, and look out the window and take in the surroundings that buzzed by as we drove on the expressway. The center that I was headed to was 10 minutes from where I grew up, so just seeing familiar places that I had not seen in what seemed like forever felt so good to me. When we arrived there was a short orientation that explained how things worked around the place along with the rules. At this point I was down to about 58 days or so until my outdate, so my countdown was all I was concerned about. I was also anxious to see how soon I would be able to get movement to walk around by myself. During the orientation I learned the unfortunate news that I would not be able to leave the facility until 2 weeks of being there. This did kind of kill some of my excitement, but I was still excited about being so close to home and my family being able to come see me more often. They still capped the number of visits you could receive, but it was much more than the 5 that I was allowed in the prison. It had been so long since I had been free, just being around people who had been coming and going on the outside really showed me how far removed I had been. I heard people talking about things like smartphones, social media, and a bunch of other stuff that I never knew existed. I would just sit down and listen as some of the younger guys brought me up to speed on what type of stuff was going on outside of this place. I was so anxious to get my movement, but also cautious as they made it clear that they did not hesitate to send you back to the prison should you go outside of the boundaries set forth. There were also a couple of the staff that were similar to some of the guards back in the prison, mad at the world for whatever reason and they did their best to ruin whatever happiness they seen in anyone and found excitement in seeing people get sent back. I made it my point to do my best to stay away from these people as best I could. I had one foot in and one foot out the door, so I definitely was not trying to blow this as it was much better than sitting my last couple of months in prison.

Once I was finally able to get movement, I was supposed to only go out to my prescheduled places to look for employment that were approved by my counselor. Most of the guys in the place had already given me the run down on how things worked there. They would say they were going out to look for jobs, but would pretty much so go wherever they wanted, just making sure they did not get caught. Some guys went back to their neighborhoods to sell drugs, smoke weed, drink with their friends, along with a bunch of other stuff that would clearly get them sent back. There were a couple of instances where people came back and had to take a random drug test, failed, and were immediately sent back. Maybe it was because a lot of these guys were younger and had only spent maybe a month or so in actual prison before being granted work release, so they did not take it very seriously. With me having spent pretty much so my entire sentence locked up, going through everything that I had over the years, I definitely was not in a rush to get sent back. Over the short 2 weeks I had been there it was already one of the guards that made it clear that he did not like me and he would do whatever it took to get me sent back. Again, there was the impression I must have unknowingly gave off that I felt I was better than the others because I was not wild, struggling, and making a fool of myself like some of my peers who were close in age to myself. At this point I was 25yrs old, spent pretty much so my entire early 20's incarcerated, so yes, I did mature a lot faster than some of the other guys they wanted me to behave like. I did not have the luxury of joking around, taking risks, no, I had kids that needed me and I actually took things very seriously. I made sure when I left the facility that I covered my tracks and went to the places that I was expected to go to. I would just knock out my agenda quickly and have my girlfriend Crystal meet me so we could spend time together while I was out. It felt so good being able to hold her, touch her, talk to her, all without numerous people watching our every move. I actually started to feel as if I was free and at that point I was ready to go home and be free completely.

During my time in the work release center, I did my best to avoid trouble, and I even started cutting hair for the guys who were going on interviews and whatnot since I had taught myself over the years being locked up. I wouldn't charge them much, if anything, as a lot of them really did not have much money, and it pretty much so helped pass the time when I was not able to move around. It had gotten to a point where the counselor stopped all of my outside movement completely, and his reason for doing so was that I was going home in a couple of weeks. I knew him and the officer that did not like me were friends, so I am pretty sure that influenced his decision. That is one thing I noticed over the duration of my incarceration, a lot of the staff have a lot of personal issues going on in their lives, and what they do is bring those same issues to work with them and take it out on the inmates because they are not in much of a position to speak out for fear of making their time harder than it has to be. With me that was a challenge I faced throughout my incarceration, it was just so hard for me to keep quiet when I knew I was being harassed by people who would never dare to do some of the stuff they did to me had I not been incarcerated. It was flat out bullying and I hated it, and because of me not being afraid to speak out I dealt with a lot of harassment. I was fed up though, and with me being so close to going home I did not want to jeopardize that, but I also was not going to be treated any type of way, especially from some the low life staff that could easily be in the same position I was in at the time. A lot of them struggled financially, some came to work drunk, and others had been through numerous divorces, among other things, so they were human just like the inmates were, but since they worked there they felt like they could come to work to take their frustrations out on us. The day before my release date, the guard who did not like me did not know it was my last night and as usual he was trying to pick with me. I was working in the kitchen at the time and he came in to get his lunch, not knowing I was in the back cooking. I watched him through the door eat his entire lunch and as soon as he finished I came out and walked past him. I looked him right in the eyes and said, "Hope you enjoyed that special meal I made for you" and I started laughing to myself as I walked away. He was furious to say the least; not knowing what I may have did to the food he just devoured. I actually did not even know he would eat in the kitchen that day, so there was nothing done to the food, but the thought alone manipulated his mind into believing so and he was pissed! He demanded that the head officer in charge send me back for poisoning his food, saying I needed to be brought up on charges for trying to poison an officer. The reality of it was that he had no proof, so there was nothing they could do to me. The other officers really did not like him anyways, so some of them laughed at him and this only made him even more upset. As much as I should not have done that, the guy had it coming to him and it made my day just seeing him as mad as he was. I felt it was a victory for all of the inmates he had harassed over the years, and everyone laughed at him for the rest of the day. As much as that pleased me, little did I know he would get the opportunity to get me back one last time.

Early the next morning I was called down to get ready to go home. Finally, the words I had been waiting to hear for 48 months were finally spoke over the intercom, "Cummings, get your property and come to the front desk so you can get processed out to go home". The excitement that I was feeling slowly diminished as I came to find out the officer that did not like me had worked a double shift and had now found out I was going home. He came in over the intercom and told me that he would let me out when he felt like it. I was livid! My mom had already told me that she would be there bright and early to pick me up, not letting anyone come with her because she wanted to be the first person to spend time with me when I got out. As the time passed, I sat at the door holding my property, waiting for this guy to buzz me out, getting angrier as each minute passed. As angry as I had gotten, I kept a smile on my face looking him eye to eye in the camera as he stared me down, not letting him get the satisfaction of seeing me get upset. This was my day and I would not let anyone ruin it. After about an hour of the awkward stare down between us another officer finally buzzed me out. As I walked out of that front door I kept a smile on my face, staring at him the entire time walking out the front door, and as petty as it was I gave him my middle finger, leaving no doubt in anyone's mind as to how I felt about him. As the door closed behind me I could hear him scream, "You'll be back". Little did he know I was on a mission, and coming back to prison was not on the agenda at all! He did get the last laugh though, because when I came out front there was no one waiting for me. My mom was nowhere in sight. The way I was feeling I did not care if I had to walk home, there was no way I was going back into that place, not even to use the phone to call her. As I walked up the street, carrying all of my property in two duffel bags, I saw my mom turn the corner driving in my direction. She pulled on the side of me, asking why was I walking up the street like this. I told her what happened with the guard and she informed me that he had told her that my paperwork was behind and I would not be released until later that afternoon, so she went up the street to get some coffee. I just laughed to myself, my mom and I hugging in the middle of the street, refusing to let each other go. With tears falling down her cheeks she told me that I better not ever put her through that again, and right there I promised her that not only would we never go through that again, but it was now time again for me to make my family proud.

While I was in the work release center, a friend of my dads had a son who was a co-owner of a metal recycling company, so he told him that he could get me a job as a laborer working there once I was released. This was good because the state had recently passed legislation within the Department of Corrections to help ease the overcrowding of the prisons and also help decrease the workload of the probation and parole officers. If you came out of the work release center, got employment, and stayed out of trouble, then they would cut your parole time down tremendously. With my particular case, I was set to have 3yrs of parole, so I was definitely going to do whatever I had to in order to get that time cut down. It took about a week or so for me to hear from my parole officer, and it was only due to me calling repeatedly every other day informing them that I needed to see him so I could start a job that was waiting on me, that she arranged a meeting for me to come see her. When we met she informed me that if I stayed out of trouble, kept a steady job, and did not catch any dirty drops (drug tests), then I could get my parole cut down to 6 months. I told her that she had nothing to worry about; I was a man on a mission and had things to accomplish. Sensing my determination she assured me that I would be fine.

After being free a couple of weeks, I started my new job and I also went to the community college and enrolled to start the upcoming semester with a full-time course load. My mind was focused on spending time with my family, going to work, hitting the gym, and going to school. There were several people that I had not heard from in years trying to reach out to me and looking to hang out, but I would constantly decline stating I just did not have the free time to do so. In my mind, they were not there for me when I went through one of the lowest points in my life, so at this point I was only focused on being around the people who were there for me. Crystal and I came to find out that she was pregnant from one of our days spent together while I was at the work release center, so that definitely was unexpected. I did not want to be put back in the same situation I had been in previously, doing whatever to support my family. We decided that we would not only work together to make it work, but I told her I would do things right this time. Not wanting to have yet anther child out of wedlock, I took some of the money I had saved up and went to buy her an engagement ring, and one day surprised her as I proposed to her. After all that we had been through, all that I had put her through over the years, I wanted her to see how serious I was about us building a family together, and also building a future together. I made a promise to her while I was away, and though a lot of family and others tried to say it was merely "prison talk", I definitely was serious. I was not expecting to add another child to the mix so soon with me just coming home, but I felt it was a blessing and we would make it work.

After getting a routine established of me going to work full-time, going to school full-time, taking time out to be with my family, I felt it was time for me to find a church to attend so that I could stay focused spiritually. I was keeping myself together physically by going to the gym daily, I was keeping myself together mentally by going to school and continuously educating myself, so it was now time to get on track spiritually. A good friend of mine that I grew up with invited me to go with her to church one Sunday. The service was pretty good, so I went a couple of times with her. I really did not feel like that was the right place for me, so another friend of mine asked me if I wanted to go with her to visit her church on a Saturday evening. It was a well-known church on the south side of the city name Salem Baptist Church of Chicago that was pastored by Rev. James Meeks, one of those mega church type places. The Saturday service that we went to was at the smaller location, so we weren't in the big building that they hold the Sunday services in. As the pastor spoke that night, it was almost as if he was speaking directly to me. The sermon was on changing your life, getting out of bad habits, and it touched on a lot of points that I could definitely relate to. With me growing up not going to a church like this, it was a challenge for me to block out the people screaming, running laps full speed around the place, and a lot of other actions that I was not used to being around when trying to get educated about God. I still received the message that night, and I actually felt like this was a place I would like to stick around for a while. That night I joined the church, and I felt like things were starting to become complete in my life now that the spiritual aspect was being fulfilled.

Since I had already been attending college before and during my incarceration, it did not take me long to finish up my Associate's degree. I had so many credits at that point; I was able to graduate with two Associate degrees, so I wanted to keep going. I had made some very aggressive goals while in prison, so I started applying to some universities so that I could pursue my Bachelors degree. I was very excited when I received the news that I was accepted to Chicago State University, and I would be starting the upcoming semester. At this point at my job, things were not going so well for me. I had started experiencing severe foot pain with me being on my feet all day wearing steel toe boots, and some days it was difficult for me to even walk. I associated this with the fact that I had not done any type strenuous work like this for over the last 5yrs of my life, so my body was not allowing me to continue the job much longer. The guy that had initially got me the job had gotten along very well with me, and he knew I was going to school full-time in addition to supporting my family, so he moved me to another position at the place that would allow me to not be on my feet so much. He always would tell me that he really liked my work ethic, and really respected me for what I was doing considering where I had just come from, so he told me he would always try to help me as much as he could. There was a major recession in the economy while I was incarcerated, and the affects of it was still present in a lot of industries even when I came home a few years later. It had taken its toll on the company I was working for, so a lot of people had to get laid off towards the end of my first year working there, and since I was just recently hired, I was on the list to get laid off, but they told us that we would be able to get unemployment benefits. As much as I hated the fact of me no longer receiving a steady paycheck, I felt it was a sign for me to take the initiative to start my own business, and that is what I did.

One of the businesses that I researched and wrote a business plan for while incarcerated was a coin operated vending machine business. I had some money saved up, so I found a company that built the machines, and they would also place the machines in locations for you. I wanted to start off slow, but I didn't want to be afraid to take a chance, so I initially was going to purchase 50 machines. I started getting a bad vibe from the company I was dealing with, so I ended up telling them that I would only start with 30 machines, see how things went, then add more as I seen necessary. The company did not like the fact that I no longer wanted to purchase all of the machines, so the relationship turned very sour. They started taking their time to place the machines I paid for, and when my attorney threatened them with legal action they placed the machines, but they screwed me over in the process. They went into a very bad part of the city and went into several businesses telling them that the machines were for charity and would only be there for 30 days, so this presented a problem for me because the goal was have the machines placed in long term locations, and them lying to the business owners saying that it was for charity caused a lot of confusion when I finally showed up to visit each of the machine locations. There were several companies that told me to remove the machines, a few places stole the machines and told me they never received them, and there was just a lot of confusion. I can say I was thankful for the business owners that allowed me to keep my machines in their businesses because they seen that I was a young black male just trying to do some positive stuff, not getting into trouble like a lot of my peers in the neighborhood that surrounded their businesses. I learned that in business I would have to do a better job of researching the people, and companies, that I choose to business with in the future. This situation was not ideal, but I had money invested in it at this point so I told myself to just hang in there and make the best out of it.

Since I had been laid off, I had set up everything with the unemployment benefits and I also went to apply for food stamps to help me out until I got back on my feet. I can honestly say that with this being my first time ever applying for any type of government assistance, it was a very humbling experience. A lot of the staff were very rude, and just seemed so angry with everyone each time I needed to go to the office. I made a promise to myself that I would get something going as soon as possible because I hated dealing with the entire process. I would constantly have to visit the employment office since I was attending school at the time, waiting several hours to been seen, dealing with attitudes from the staff each time, and I was just becoming more frustrated trying to get things done. I was staying with my parents at the time with the goal to move into my own place at the start of the New Year. Before I went away, I had some money that I left with my mom and she ended up using it, in conjunction with some of her own resources, to buy a house not too far from where they lived. During the time I was away she rented it out to family, fixed it up, and it was all so I could have a place to live once I was released. I was very appreciative of her for that, making sure my daughters and I would have a place to stay once I came home. I knew the unemployment would not be enough to survive on, and with the vending business just being started, I couldn't depend on that income since things were still trying to come together, so I decided I would start my own landscaping business. With me having a lot of experience working in the yard from my childhood, I figured this would be a good business venture that could help bring in some more money.

I had some money saved up, so I purchased a used pickup truck and some other used lawn care equipment. From there I printed up some fliers and passed them around the neighborhood, gave them out to my family, friends, and anyone else I knew. I wanted to start off slow since I was still going to school, so I was able to pick up a small number of customers that first year to maintain their lawns. At this point I was going to school full-time, which was not as hard as I thought it would be. I found out that Chicago State was not really a good fit for me, so while enrolled I started applying to some more reputable universities because I wanted to go somewhere that would not only challenge me, but also have a strong reputation so once I finished it could help me find employment. While at Chicago State I did meet some very good people, some of whom I still frequently communicate with today. I was going to church faithfully each week, and I started volunteering to feed the homeless in our neighborhood once a week. I really enjoyed this because I had a strong desire to give back, and it also put me around people that I was able to give hope by telling them my testimony. Things were going well for me, and I can say I was truly thankful. During this time I recently had my youngest daughter, Crystal and I had gotten married, so we had moved into our first home together and things looked bright for both our futures. I have to admit, money was not like it used to be back when I was selling drugs, and at times it was very challenging for us financially, but I always kept praying, and I was satisfied with making an honest living and being free. People in my neighborhood that knew me from the past could not understand how I went from selling drugs, living the fast life and having a good time, to pushing a old lawn mower across people's yards in 90-100 degree temperatures. They did not understand why I went to school full-time, declining to go out and party, and instead stay up late at the library doing homework, writing papers. No, they did not understand, and I did not expect them to. This was my vision, and I knew what I wanted out of my life. I was the only one who had lived each day in that prison throughout all of those years, so no, I did not expect anyone to understand why I did what I was doing, and honestly I did not care. The people I cared about supported me and that was all that mattered. I did not expect things to be easy when I was released, but failure was not an option for me at this point.

CHAPTER 10: LIFE LESSONS TO GET

YOU TO MUCH SUCCESS

The day I was accepted into Saint Xavier University was one of the happiest days of my life. Not only is the university very well known, but I felt getting a degree from a prestigious school like that would increase my chances of finding a good job once I finished. I worked very hard in every course I took there, keeping consistent straight A's in all my courses, making the Dean's List, getting invited to join a special student counsel board who advised the president and other members of the business school, was inducted to Delta Mu Delta which is a national honor society for business majors, among other accomplishments while I was in attendance. I worked my landscaping business during the day, and attended evening classes four nights out of the week. I was determined to make the best out of the experience and really build my resume, so I started volunteering for a couple of organizations within the school as well. I did everything the right way, giving my all to ensure that I graduated at the top of my class so I could be recruited for jobs available within some of the big Fortune 500 companies that I had my eye on. When I got towards the last semester before I would graduate, my advisor informed me that if I completed 4 other courses then I would be able to graduate with a double major, so not only would I have my business management degree, but I would also complete the business marketing degree as well. This would force me to take 7 courses in my final semester, yes that's right-7 coursed, and though it was going to be a challenge, I knew it would look very good on my resume. I can honestly say it was not easy at all trying to juggle my landscaping business, running the plumbing business with my dad, trying to maintain several courses in the evening, all along with trying to manage time with my family. As difficult as it was, I figured if I put the time in while I was younger and had more energy, then later down the road in life things would be much easier.

During the time I was finishing up school, I had started applying to several companies in search of my dream job to start my career. I would get called on numerous interviews, sometimes 8-10 per week, but I started to notice a pattern. When I first started interviewing with companies the person(s) interviewing me would get so excited about having me join their team, often times making me job offers on the spot. I had gotten offers for management positions with salaries starting off as high as $70k per year, which me getting something like that straight out of school would have been great. Once it would come time to do the pre-employment process of taking the drug screening I would be fine. When it came down to verifying my referrals I would be great. I had gotten letters of recommendation from professors, people from my church, people I did business with, so I came highly recommended to say the least. The companies were always impressed with my resume, noticing my experience I had running my own businesses, and seeing how well I had performed at such a prestigious university, along with my volunteering experience. Each job offer came to an immediate halt when it came down to my background check though. The entire vibe would turn from excitement, looking forward to me joining their team, to sadness and disappointment, realizing that this perfect job candidate was indeed a convicted felon with a tarnished background. There was even a couple of instances where the interviewers called me crying on the phone, expressing how sad they were to hear that I had even been through something like that, because from meeting me they would never have guessed. I never let the fact of me being incarcerated define me though, and I never used it to ask for any type of preferential treatment from anyone. That's the challenge though with being an ex-convict in our society, there is such a contradictory treatment that you get from people. They want you to change your life around, do things the right way, and not let the past define you. What contradicts that though is the simple fact that most people are going to judge you, and most will be hesitant to give you a second chance. I will explain how you can overcome that and still be successful in a moment.

Even though the goal of going to school and getting my degree was to help me qualify for the type of jobs that I wanted to work in, educating yourself and obtaining knowledge is something that no one can ever take from you, so never dismiss going to school and getting an education. During the time that I was enrolled in school I would apply the principles I was learning in class in my business to see if it really worked, and I would be so excited when I would get positive results from it. Another benefit of going to school is being around people from different walks of life, and it is essential to you getting a better understanding of how the world around you works. With me going to some very diverse schools, it allowed me the opportunity to socialize with people from different cultural backgrounds, people from different social classes, and interacting with them taught me a lot in regards to not only how different people view others in society, but why they feel the way that they do. I think this was very important because in life you will deal with this same diverse environment of people, so it helps you know how to interact with people from different walks of life and still be yourself. I never changed for anyone, but from dealing with so many different people, it allowed me the confidence in knowing who I was and not being afraid to walk in my shoes each day. I knew what I had been through and I know what type of man it had built me into, so that is who I was when I interacted with anyone I met and gained lots of respect for doing so. Always be able to look yourself in the mirror and be satisfied with the person you are, and if you see that some changes need to be made then do so.

Throughout the time of me growing up, unknowingly to me at the time, I had a strong passion for business. The only bad part about that was that I was involved in illegal businesses, and from that I had to experience a lot of the challenges that I faced in life. The time I spent in prison opened my eyes to this and made me start putting my energy into learning how to build and run legitimate businesses, and going to school just taught me different conceptual ideas that I did not know existed. This is something that you will have to do if you are going to be successful. You need to evaluate what it is that you are passionate about, something that comes easy to you, and from there educate yourself so that you can get even better. The lesson I learned was that it was not meant for me to work for anyone else, and running my own business(s) is what I was destined to do. This is what I am passionate about, and this is something I enjoy doing. This passion for business, and being my own boss, is what had me humble myself and start cutting grass, shoveling snow, just like I did when I was a little kid. Little did I know that each year my landscaping business would grow, provide jobs to people with backgrounds who were in similar situations like I was and had difficulty finding employment, along with help provide me with a sustainable income that helped provide for my family. I never expected to build my landscaping business up from scratch and one day be able to put it up for sale to move on to the next phase of my life. That's the thing though, it comes down to having faith in yourself, even when so many people will place doubt on you, and never being afraid to take a chance in doing something different from what you may have been accustomed to. I could have easily given up after so many job rejections, but I kept pushing forward. It had gotten to a point when I felt so hopeless, felt so frustrated and at times thinking I would at some point be forced to go back to the life I once knew because I felt doing things the right way just was not going to work for me. This is where having a strong support system comes into play.

While attending school, I had made some solid connections with some great people that contributed to my success. Some of those relationships evolved into long-term friendships, with people who constantly motivate me to keep striving towards doing more. Surround yourself around people who have no ulterior motives, and seeing you succeed not only benefits you, but it also helps push them as well. You want to be around people who are driven and looking towards accomplishing great things in life just as you are. Never keep negative people around you; they will only influence your mind into disqualifying ever taking action to accomplish your goals. This is why you want to physically write down your goals and keep them somewhere safe, not being quick to discuss them with everyone, but putting them into action and letting your actions do all of the talking for you. This is what I did when I started writing my business plans while still incarcerated, being in one of the most negative environments that you could imagine. Everyone will not support you doing something different, and at times it will hurt when the people you care about don't support you, but do not let that stop you. This is why it was so important for me to go to school, being around people who had different thoughts and goals, because that took me out of my comfort zone of what I was accustomed to and challenged me to do something different. That's not to say that you have to cut off all of the people you love, but you will naturally see yourself start to interact with different people on different levels. The old friends that you grew up with who may still have the same mentality, you will find yourself naturally start to limit the time you spend with them because your mentality will be different. You want to allocate your time towards progressing your life, and the people you spend the most time with will greatly influence that.

Along with my wife, I was blessed to have life place one of my childhood best friends back in my life. With the help of social media, we were able to connect and realize during the time we were in different states from each other, our paths in life had a lot of similarities, which brought us to the point we were at as adults now. We both have families we are supporting, we both work very hard to improve not only our personal lives, but also looking to progress within our respective careers. We both have a desire to build a stronger relationship with God, and it just made sense for us to start motivating each other to become successful. This also relates to a former classmate that I met while at SXU, who also was very driven and over time we have built a very strong friendship as well. These are the people that I spend the majority of my time with at this point in my life, among other business associates, and we all encourage each other to keep driving, never get complacent, and we all are experiencing a life that we always thought might not be obtainable given where we came from. That's my point though, the more you build your circle around people who are just as motivated as you are to succeed, and be sure to weed out the negativity from others who have no benefit to you, then this will greatly increase your chances of becoming successful. It reminds me of the quote I once read, "Your net worth is directly related to your network." The time you invest in the people you keep around you will be directly related to your likelihood of becoming successful. Never forget this because it is so important.

During the time I was building my landscaping company, I lived a very frugal life and I was very aggressive at saving the little money I was making at the time, and I also worked hard on building my personal credit position. Since I was selling drugs before I went to jail, I never really utilized my credit with the exception of maybe a phone bill and some other small items, so unlike my peers who ruined their credit during their late teenage years and early 20's, I avoided that mistake in life. This became a very important tool for me to utilize because this contributed to me building my landscaping business. Since I had a good credit score, I was able to use that to expand my business, being able to leverage lines of credit to purchase the more expensive equipment that I needed to make my company more efficient. Be sure to take care of your credit, and make sure you always are saving money, even if it's not a lot. If you have credit issues get them fixed as soon as you can. There are several companies that specialize in helping repair credit, so research them and find one that will help you accomplish this. A small amount saved on a regular basis eventually grows into something that you will be able to use in your journey to becoming successful. I spent countless hours during my incarceration reading books on how to build credit, what the interest rates meant, how the credit score system worked and its importance, among other things of value. This also was another benefit I gained from going to school, as I was able to learn from other people who had been taught growing up about credit and saving by their parents. Unfortunately, in a lot of minority households subjects like credit, saving money, and other related topics do not get taught very often, so you end up getting caught in the trap of unknowingly dismissing the importance of these items and it puts you in a position in life that can prevent you from being able to have any type of success. If your credit is not good, then this prevents you from obtaining loans to buy a home, a car, or anything else for that matter. If you include also the fact of not saving money, then this can easily create a barrier to you ever becoming successful. Take the time to educate yourself on both these topics and other important financial topics so that you can know the importance of them and how they can be used to get you to the next level.

In addition to saving money and learning about the importance of credit, you will also need to learn how to invest the money that you save. I won't get too far into the many different types of investing, but one I will touch on here is investing in real estate, in addition to small business investments. When I was first released from prison and started working that first job, I had a goal to save the majority of my paycheck each week and start building my saving accounts. Even though it was not a lot of money, I took advantage of the fact that I was living with my parents at the time and did not have a lot of financial obligations. I helped as much as I could with my kids financially, helped with what I was able to around my parent's house, and I did not go out much at all. This not only put me in a position to invest in my vending machine business, but it also put me in a much better position when I was laid off from my then job, and gave me the funds to invest in my landscaping business. Even though I had to start off very small, had I not been saving my money I would not have been able to have the funds I needed to purchase the equipment I started my company with. This also brings me to the point of investing in real estate. Over the years I had the landscaping company, I continued to save on a regular basis and also focused on maintaining low debt levels to keep a good credit score. The vending business had gotten to a point where I was not generating a strong enough income to convince me to keep running it, so I liquidated all of what was left of the machines and invested that money into my landscaping business as well. This all contributed to me being able to keep building my landscaping business, and it also allowed me to pay off the equipment and small business loans that were associated with the landscaping business. Keeping good credit and good saving reserves is even more important for small business owners because unexpected expenses can always occur, often times at the worst possible time, so being able to have access to funds outside of your savings is important.

With me having a solid network of my best friends, we decided to invest in our first real estate project. We found a beat-up house in a very affluent suburb outside of Chicago and purchased it to rehab and resale it. I had read countless books on rehabbing residential properties while in prison, and I had watched even more TV shows on the topic, so we felt between the 3 of us we could take the chance to put what knowledge we did have at the time into motion and make this happen. I had gotten to a point where I was ready to put what I learned into action, if not, I would be just learning for the rest of my life and never take the step to make it happen. Needless to say, there was a lot that we found out that we did not know, and the project did not go the way we had planned. It got to the point where we wanted to just get out of this project, take whatever losses we had endured, and walk away with a lot of knowledge from the experience. I was able to come across an investment strategy that allowed me to sell the property without doing any of the repairs, and it netted us a profit as opposed to the loss we were anticipating. Getting that first check got me excited and I started to get more serious about learning this business. After that I started attending more networking events so that I could meet more people in the business with experience, all with the intention of learning more from them and possibly finding a mentor. I went to school to get my real estate license, and from there I started my company SunShyne Realty Group. Each year my company continued to grow, and the more I networked with other people in the business, the more I copied the blueprint of successful companies that I wanted to grow into, and I could see consistent growth within my company. Each year I did more transactions, and each year my team grew. I started to see that my real estate business not only generated more profit than my landscaping business, but it was also less stressful and allowed me to start living a life I did not know existed before. With the landscaping business I created myself a job that I had 100% control over, and I was blessed to be able to have that. With the real estate company though, I actually have a business, and this business allows me to work remotely, and also has the opportunity for me to operate in any part of the country that I choose. After my third year in the real estate business, I sold my landscaping business so that I could focus on building my company full-time, so I took all of the proceeds from that sale and put it all into real estate. My goal is to gradually re-build the South Side of Chicago one house at a time. I want to take the unsafe, run down properties that present potential dangers to my community, and I will renovate them to provide quality housing that is affordable to the people who have a desire to own their own property in their neighborhoods. With me now at 32 years of age as I write this, I will accomplish the goal I set for myself of retiring by the time I'm in my mid to late 40's if I continue on the path that I am on right now. Not too bad for the ex-con that all of the companies refused to take a chance on.

As I look back on everything, I believe the most import contributions to my growing success came from me having a very solid support system, and most importantly building a very close relationship with God. Now that I would have never imagined, especially coming from the former atheist who stopped even believing that God existed. That is the big reason why I am telling my story, yes, I want to motivate people to be overcome the obstacles in life and experience success in their lives, but that is not the main reason. With me having so much potential, being so intelligent, as so many people around the world are, my surroundings almost sucked me in and made me just another statistic. I think back to all of the positive men locked up in prison for the rest of their lives, many with so many talents, who could have been anything they wanted to had they not gotten sucked in by their circumstances. I was given a second chance, and I believe I went through everything that I did because God seen the potential in me, and I was just too hard headed to change on my own, so he had me experience something very severe to get my attention and wake me up. For many others out there, it could be a variety of other situations that wake you up such as homelessness, someone close to you dying, you overcoming a terminal illness, and the list goes on. Sometimes we have to experience something severe in life to wake us up so that we can realize our purpose here on this earth and not blow it. I am here to say that anything is possible, coming from someone who hit rock bottom in life, only to gain strength from it and now be blessed enough to experience so much success, and I am far from being finished. I continue to pass my blessings along to others, always trying to help others in need, providing my resources to family and strangers alike, never expecting anything in return. That is how you will be blessed. Never be the person who is reluctant to give back, but pass your blessings along to others and just watch how God will bless you. I am so thankful to have a loving family, be in good health, have a successful business that is consistently growing, and most of all, I am thankful to be a survivor of the American prison system and be able to motivate others. I hope my story reaches someone and helps him or her to overcome whatever obstacle or challenge they may be facing. If that happens, then I am truly indeed blessed. Thanks for reading my story.

ABOUT THE AUTHOR

To those that know him most, Larmon Cummings Jr has always had a passion for business. When he was young he would rake leaves, shovel snow, help his dad on plumbing jobs, and was never afraid to work hard in order to earn money and get whatever it was he set his heart on. Though his business aspirations went wayward with him selling drugs as his chosen business venture, the success he had doing so still made it evident that his passion for business would lead him towards a lot of success-he just needed to get back on track and head in the right direction. As challenging as the incarceration was on him, that was the best thing that could've happened in his life. That experience made him do a serious self-evaluation of where his life was going, and then and there he made the decision to get it together and do something different with himself. The incarceration helped him also re-establish his relationship with God, and from there he has never looked back. He made the decision that he needed to change his life in order for him to be a better man for his family, for his community, and most importantly for himself.

Upon his release, Larmon explored several entrepreneurial endeavors, but he found a passion for real estate and has been able to use his natural business talents to become not only very successful in his own life, but also pass that knowledge along to others in order for them to create better lives for themselves and their families as well. Larmon has grown a real passion for giving back to his community by volunteering, mentoring, and anything else that can have a positive impact on the world. He hopes this book will continue to aide in his efforts to make a positive change in the world, along with motivate others to make the best out of the rest of their lives, no matter what challenges and obstacles they may have faced in the past.

Made in the USA
Monee, IL
28 January 2020